$2-50

PHILOSOPHICAL ANALYSIS

An Introduction to Its Language and Techniques

Studies in Philosophy

Consulting Editor: V. C. CHAPPELL · *The University of Chicago*

PHILOSOPHICAL ANALYSIS

An Introduction to Its Language and Techniques

Second Edition

Samuel Gorovitz

Ron G. Williams

Donald Provence

Merrill Provence

Random House · New York

Preface to the Second Edition

In revising the first edition, we have given particular attention to the logical notions introduced in the first three chapters and to the notation used to develop them. We have introduced several changes designed to make our remarks clearer and more precise. Several other sections have been revised in order to add new material or elucidate the old, and minor changes are widespread throughout the book. Nevertheless, we have held to the original aims expressed in the preface to the first edition and the introduction—especially to the conviction that the book is best viewed as a starting point and not as a definitive handbook.

Exercises have been added to most chapters to provide the student with opportunity for practice in using the material presented.

We have profited from discussion and correspondence with many colleagues whose useful suggestions for improvement have aided us in making revisions. Particular thanks go to Professors Nino Cocchiarella and Rolf Sartorius, and to Mr. William Thomas, for valuable suggestions, which have resulted in many of the changes and corrections in this edition.

Preface

Students beginning the study of history, literature, or physics have for the most part a roughly accurate idea of the nature of the subject matter they are about to confront. So it is with most fields. But students beginning the study of analytic philosophy have in general no idea at all what sort of discipline they are about to encounter. This lack of knowledge presents the instructor with an additional burden—one which is not easy to overcome. For the question of the nature of philosophy is itself a philosophical issue, which can be handled properly only when the students have—or perhaps are in the process of developing—some competence in philosophy. It is in the interest of advancing the development of such competence that this book was written.

The book was conceived during the course of an informal seminar on the teaching of philosophy organized by a group of Stanford graduate students. Part of the purpose of this seminar was to develop a rather detailed syllabus for the kind of introductory philosophy course that the members of the group believed they would like to teach. The consensus was that a beginning student should be given the opportunity to study a few basic philosophical problems in depth. It was decided that treatment of a few problems in depth could best be accomplished if the student were first given a concise introduction to the language of modern philosophy. No adequate written material for such an introduction was available.

This book is thus aimed at what the authors consider to be a specific need. We intend the book to provide the materials for a program of familiarization with the language and techniques of analytic philosophy, for students who have had no prior acquaintance with the discipline.

No attempt has been made to write a comprehensive survey of any sort. The topics that are included in this volume were chosen as being most relevant to the type of problem the authors wish to treat in their own courses. However, most of the topics discussed are so basic to modern philosophical analysis that they should be relevant to many different types of courses. In addition, we have attempted to include material that will help the student avoid what, in our experience, are the mistakes most commonly made by beginning students in philosophy.

This book provides no final word and is no substitute for solid philosophical inquiry. Its purpose will be defeated if it is viewed as a compendium of philosophical method. Moreover, there is a serious danger inherent in the very nature of this book; any compact presentation of techniques and distinctions can, merely by its existence, give the impression that the problems of the discipline in question can be met simply by drawing upon a previously developed arsenal of procedures. Yet any such impression of philosophical inquiry is grossly in error. In fact, the distinctions and techniques described here, like all those in philosophy, arose out of confrontation with substantive issues and were developed in the light of new problems. Yet to justify the distinctions we discuss by presenting an historical account of their development would defeat the purpose for which the book was conceived. We have, therefore, tried to motivate the development of the material in a natural way, but the major task in this respect lies in the hands of the instructor.

The various sections of the book are, insofar as possible, independent of one another. Where there is dependence, the relevant sections are cited. Thus, sections may be omitted or used in a different sequence at the option of the instructor.

The authors wish to acknowledge their indebtedness to the Philosophy Department at Stanford University for encouragement, advice, and material support in connection with this project. We wish also to thank the other members of the seminar, Marcia Muelder Eaton, Hugh Petrie, Terry Parsons, David Howell, and John Wallace, for their help in planning this book and for their criticisms of it. Michael Rohr was very helpful in the preparation of the bibliography. Professor Vere Chappell, as the publisher's advisor, provided valuable encouragement and evaluation throughout. Finally, our thanks are due to the many people in various fields who have provided constructive suggestions for the improvement of the manuscript.

Introduction

Philosophy is a discipline relatively free of technical language and specialized methods. Whereas the problems of modern physics, for example, can be appreciated only by those trained in advanced mathematics and experimental techniques, many of the most fundamental problems of philosophy can be stated in rather simple terms.

There are, however, certain concepts that find their primary use in philosophical discourse, and there are certain techniques—particularly those of symbolic logic—that are commonly employed by philosophers. This book is designed to acquaint beginning students in philosophy with the most basic of these concepts and methods. A mastery of the material presented here should enable the student to progress more rapidly in his study of philosophy and to treat on a deeper level the philosophical questions he encounters. Such mastery can, of course, be gained only by a careful reading and rereading of the sections that follow.

The authors have attempted to give an impartial presentation of certain key terms and procedures—that is, a presentation which does not express a particular philosophical position. But this attempt is bound to fail, at least at some points, because virtually no interesting discussion of a basic

concept is noncontroversial, nor does any method have the
approval of all philosophers. Therefore, we cannot overem-
phasize the point that this book does not provide any final
word on philosophical method. To treat the book as a philosophical dictionary, or as an authoritative discourse on
methods of analysis, can only lead to trouble. No list of techniques is a substitute for careful analysis and uninhibited
thinking. Hence, the intended use of this book is as a starting point for a painstaking examination of the problems of
philosophy—an examination which, if pursued with dili-
gence, will surely lead to a reappraisal of the material presented here.

Contents

PHILOSOPHICAL ANALYSIS

An Introduction to Its Language and Techniques

I

Elementary Logic

1. Introduction

The study of logic has, for over 2000 years, engaged the interest of both those who wish to gain practical advantage from a knowledge of the principles of reasoning and those who pursue the subject for its own sake. The practical benefits of this study are undeniable. Those with an interest in increasing, organizing, or using knowledge have turned to logic—from the early Greek philosophers to the men from many fields who together developed modern computer science on the basis of their knowledge of formal logic. Moreover, logic, as it develops, becomes an increasingly important and intriguing theoretical discipline. By no means a static 'body of knowledge' that exists to be learned and used, logic is a viable and creative field, in many ways similar to and connected with mathematics.

For philosophers, the study of logic provides a means of facilitating the attempt to develop well-argued positions and to evaluate critically the positions espoused by others. The material that follows is not designed to give the reader any significant mastery of the techniques of formal logic. Rather, it is aimed at facilitating communication—at enabling the reader to understand the use of logic that he will come across as he begins to be exposed, in the classroom or in the literature, to a contemporary analytical approach to philosophical problems.

2. *Arguments, Validity, and Truth*

We may consider logic to be an analysis of the structure of reasoning. We encounter reasoning in the form of arguments. An argument, considered from the viewpoint of formal logic, is a set of sentences, one of which is claimed to be a conclusion that follows from the others. Thus:

> (1) All men are bipeds.
> A   (2) Edgar is a man.
> (3) (Therefore) Edgar is a biped.

is an argument in which line $A(3)$ is the conclusion that follows from lines $A(1)$ and $A(2)$. If we know $A(1)$ and $A(2)$, we can deduce that $A(3)$ is true. Lines $A(1)$ and $A(2)$ are called premises; line $A(3)$ is called the conclusion.

Consider the following three lines:

> (1) All men are bipeds.
> B   (2) George is a man.
> (3) (Therefore) Rover is a biped.

Here, too, we have an argument, which resembles A in form. But this time we notice something strange. The purported conclusion, line $B(3)$, does not follow from the premises at all. Even if we know $B(1)$ and $B(2)$ to be true, we can still deny $B(3)$. So B, like A, is an argument; but B, unlike A, is not a good argument. Its conclusion does not follow from its premises, and we call such arguments invalid.

I may know that no one in San Francisco is seven feet tall and that John Jones is a five-foot New Yorker. Still, I can assert that if it *were* true that all San Franciscans are seven feet tall and that John Jones lives in San Francisco, then it would follow that John Jones is seven feet tall. The argument would look like this:

       (1) All San Franciscans are seven feet tall.
C   (2) John Jones is a San Franciscan.
       (3) (Therefore) John Jones is seven feet tall.

Argument *C*, like argument *A*, is valid; that is, both arguments are such that it must be that if the premises are true, the conclusion is true. The conclusion of a valid argument is a logical consequence of its premises, and the premises are said to imply or to entail the conclusion. But *C*, unlike *A*, has false premises. Thus, we see that a sentence can be the conclusion of a valid argument and still be false. For, to say that a sentence is the conclusion of a valid argument is to say only that it must be true *if* the premises of the argument are true. But consider *D*:

       (1) All men are mortal.
D   (2) Socrates is a man.
       (3) (Therefore) John Jones is seven feet tall.

Here the conclusion clearly does not follow. It is invalid. Yet *D*(3) is the same sentence as *C*(3). That sentence is both the conclusion of a valid argument and the conclusion of an invalid argument. It is helpful in beginning the study of philosophy to speak only of arguments, not of sentences, as being valid or invalid and to speak only of sentences as being true or false.

To illustrate further the difference between truth and validity, let us consider the following arguments:

(1) All men are mortal.   (1) All women are
                                      Greeks.
E (2) Caesar is a man.   F (2) Caesar is a woman.
  (3) Caesar is mortal.   (3) Caesar is a Greek.

  (1) All men are Greeks.   (1) All men are Romans.
G (2) Caesar is a man.   H (2) Caesar is the
  (3) Caesar is a Greek.   emperor.
                                 (3) Caesar is a Greek.

  (1) All men are fish.   (1) All men are mortal.
I (2) Lassie is a man.   J (2) Caesar is a man.
  (3) Lassie is a dog.   (3) Caesar is a Roman.

We note that *E* is a valid argument with true premises
and a true conclusion. *F* is a valid argument with false premises and a false conclusion. *G* is a valid argument with one
false premise, one true premise, and a false conclusion. *H* is
an invalid argument, which, however, is just like *G* in having
a false first premise, a true second premise, and a false
conclusion. *I* is an invalid argument with false premises
and a true conclusion, and *J* is an invalid argument in spite
of the fact that both the premises and the conclusion are
true. (Compare *J* with *E* in this respect.) We can sche-
matize the situation thus, using 'T' for 'true', 'F' for 'false',
'V' for 'valid', and 'I' for 'invalid':

	T			F	
E	T		F	F	
	T	V		F	V
	F			F	
G	T		H	T	
	F	V		F	I

$$
I \quad
\begin{array}{l}
\text{F} \\
\text{F} \\
\text{T} \quad \text{I}
\end{array}
\qquad
J \quad
\begin{array}{l}
\text{T} \\
\text{T} \\
\text{T} \quad \text{I}
\end{array}
$$

We shall call an argument *sound* when it is a valid argument with true premises. Note that every sound argument must have a true conclusion, since to say that an argument is sound is to say that (1) the conclusion is true if the premises are true and (2) the premises *are* true. We can thus challenge the soundness of an argument either by questioning the truth of the premises or by questioning the validity of the argument.

Not all arguments are of the three-line form we have been considering. And not all arguments which are of that form appear at first glance to be so. For example:

K
(1) Caesar is emperor.

(2) (Therefore) Someone is emperor.

is a simple argument which is sound but has a different form. And:

L
(1) Jones is a man.

(2) (Therefore) Jones is mortal.

is an argument which is valid only on the strength of the suppressed (or unexpressed) premise that all men are mortal. Such an argument is clearly valid, and of the familiar three-line form, *if* we add the missing premise. If we do not, we can consider the argument as incomplete rather than invalid.

To sum up: An argument is a sequence of sentences, one of which (usually, but not always, the last) is claimed to

follow from the others. The one that is claimed to follow
is the conclusion; the others are the premises. An argument
is valid if and only if the conclusion is a logical consequence of the premises. An argument is sound if and only
if it is valid and has true premises.

These remarks apply only to *deductive* arguments. It
could also be said of valid deductive arguments that the
conclusion contains no information which is not contained
in the premises. Of course the content of the premises may
not be *obvious*. In *inductive* arguments the information
contained in the conclusion goes beyond that contained in
the premises, and consequently the truth of the premises
does not guarantee that the conclusion of an inductive
argument is true even though it may be a good argument.
For example:

> M   All twenty cows inoculated with Smith's vaccine
> promptly died.
> (Therefore) Smith's vaccine is fatal to all cows.

Here it is possible for the premise to be true and the
conclusion false, yet we accept the conclusion on the basis
of the premise. The analysis of such inductive inferences
is complex indeed and goes far beyond the scope of our
present concerns.

3. *Propositional Logic*

Let us now consider some of the basic features of symbolic logic, a discipline that, in addition to performing other
functions, provides techniques for determining both the
validity of some kinds of argument and the consistency of
sets of sentences.

Above, we used 'T' or 'F' to indicate the truth or falsity

of sentences in arguments *E–J*. Let us now adopt this notation officially and think of each declarative sentence as having a truth value, T or F: T, when the sentence is true; F, when the sentence is false.

Consider the sentences 'New York is the most populous city in the U.S.A.' and 'San Francisco is in Illinois'. We shall let the capital letters 'P', 'Q', and 'R' (with or without subscripts) serve as abbreviations for English sentences, allowing each letter to abbreviate only one sentence in any given context. Here, let 'P' abbreviate the sentence 'New York is the most populous city in the U.S.A.' and let 'Q' abbreviate 'San Francisco is in Illinois'. The sentence abbreviated by 'P' is true; so it has the truth value T. The sentence abbreviated by 'Q' is false and so has the truth value F. But the sentence 'New York is not the most populous city in the U.S.A.' is not true. We can rewrite this sentence, changing the words but not the meaning: 'It is not the case that New York is the most populous city in the U.S.A.' By taking advantage of our abbreviation, we may put this sentence more briefly: 'It is not the case that P'. We now have a method for creating from any declarative sentence and the phrase 'it is not the case that' a new sentence, which is said to be the *negation* of the sentence which follows the phrase 'it is not the case that'. By letting a short wavy stroke '∼' represent this phrase, we may abbreviate 'It is not the case that P' by '∼P'; and we may abbreviate 'It is not the case that San Francisco is in Illinois' by '∼Q'.[1]

Because we wish to talk about characteristics that all sentences having the same logical form have in common, we shall use Greek letters in order to talk about the logical

---

[1] '∼' is also used to represent stylistic variants of 'it is not the case that', such as 'not', 'it is not true that', and 'it is false that'.

form of sentences. Thus, if Φ is any sentence, then the result of writing '~' followed by Φ is the negation of Φ. Where Φ is any sentence, we exhibit the form of the negation of Φ by:

$$\sim\Phi.$$

Obviously if Φ is a true sentence, then ~Φ is a false sentence;[2] and if Φ is false, then ~Φ is true. We can illustrate these features of negation with the following diagram, called a truth table:

	Φ	~Φ
1	T	F
2	F	T

This table is the truth table for negation. Rows 1 and 2 represent the only possibilities for the truth value of any sentence Φ; either Φ is true or it is false, and it is not both. The second column shows that when Φ is true (first column, row 1), then ~Φ is false and that when Φ is false (first column, row 2), then ~Φ is true. On the basis of this truth table, we can see that the negation of the false sentence 'San Francisco is in Illinois' is true and that the negation of this negation, i.e., '~~Q', is false. In general, (a) Φ is true and ~Φ is false just in case ~~Φ is true; and (b) Φ is false and ~Φ is true just in case ~~Φ is false.

Now let us consider the word 'and'. By placing 'and' between any two declarative sentences, Φ and Ψ, we can form a third sentence, the conjunction of Φ and Ψ. Let-

[2] In predicating 'is a false sentence' of '~Φ' we are not being strictly correct, as the reader who further pursues the study of logic will discover. It would, however, be unnecessarily complicated for our purposes to be strictly correct in our usage of the Greek letters in combination with sentential connectives, such as '~' and parentheses. We believe that our usage will not confuse the beginning student.

ting '&' represent 'and',[3] we form the conjunction of Φ and Ψ by writing '(', followed by Φ, followed by '&', followed by Ψ, followed by ')'. That is, we exhibit the form of the conjunction of Φ and Ψ by:

$$(\Phi \,\&\, \Psi).$$

What do we know about the truth value of conjunctions? Consider the sentence 'It is raining and it is Tuesday'. This sentence is true only in case it *is* raining *and* it *is* Tuesday. Otherwise it is false. In general (Φ & Ψ) is true if Φ is true and Ψ is true; otherwise (Φ & Ψ) is false. We can illustrate the truth conditions for conjunctions with a truth table:

Φ	Ψ	(Φ & Ψ)
T	T	T
T	F	F
F	T	F
F	F	F

Here there are four rows, one for each possible combination of truth values for any two sentences Φ and Ψ.

We call '&' a sentential connective, since with it we are able to connect sentences and form new sentences. Similarly, although we do not use '∼' to *connect* sentences, we call '∼' a connective. '&' is a two-place connective—we use it between two sentences; '∼' is a one-place connective—we use it with one sentence. But of course that one sentence which is negated may itself be quite complex. When Ψ is a sentence, ∼Ψ is a sentence; so when Φ and Ψ are sentences, (Φ & ∼Ψ) is a sentence, and so also is ∼(Φ & ∼Ψ) a sentence. Notice that ∼(Φ & ∼Ψ), which

---

[3] '&' is also used to represent stylistic variants of 'and', such as 'but', 'although', 'both . . . and . . .', and 'even though'.

has the form of the negation of a conjunction, is different
from ($\sim\Phi$ & $\sim\Psi$), which has the form of a conjunction of
two negations.

Now we can form new sentences in many ways. Starting
with any sentences Φ and Ψ, we can, for example, produce
sentences of any of the following forms:

$$\sim\Phi$$
$$(\Psi \ \& \sim\Phi)$$
$$(\sim\Phi \ \& \sim\Psi)$$
$$\sim(\Phi \ \& \sim\Psi).$$

It is a simple matter to construct truth tables for any of
these; for given the truth values of any two sentences Φ
and Ψ, we can compute the truth value of any compound
produced from these sentences using our two sentential
connectives. Consider: $\sim(\Phi \ \& \sim\Psi)$.

Φ	Ψ	$\sim\Psi$	$(\Phi \ \& \sim\Psi)$	$\sim(\Phi \ \& \sim\Psi)$
T	T	F	F	T
T	F	T	T	F
F	T	F	F	T
F	F	T	F	T

Given any truth value of any sentence Ψ, we can use the
truth table for negation to compute the truth value of $\sim\Psi$.
And given any combination of truth values for Φ and $\sim\Psi$,
we can use the truth table for conjunction to compute the
truth value $(\Phi \ \& \sim\Psi)$. Finally, given any truth value
for $(\Phi \ \& \sim\Psi)$, we can use the truth table for negation once
again to compute the truth value of $\sim(\Phi \ \& \sim\Psi)$. This table
shows us the truth conditions for the negation of the conjunction of any sentence and the negation of any sentence.
It shows us that any sentence of the form $\sim(\Phi \ \& \sim\Psi)$ will

be false if Φ is true and Ψ is false; otherwise it will be true.
For example, if and only if it is raining but it is not Tuesday, the sentence 'It is not the case both that it is raining
and that it is not Tuesday' is false.

We may now consider three more sentential connectives.
We shall use 'v' to represent 'or'.[4] This connective is the
disjunction sign. The logical form of disjunctions is:

$$(\Phi \ v \ \Psi).$$

The truth table for disjunction is:

Φ	Ψ	(Φ v Ψ)
T	T	T
T	F	T
F	T	T
F	F	F

That is, if Φ and Ψ are both false sentences, then (Φ v Ψ)
is false; otherwise (Φ v Ψ) is true. Disjunction as characterized by this truth table may be said to be inclusive, in
that the disjunction is true if both of the disjuncts are true.
For example, 'Either it will rain today or it will snow today'
is true if it will both rain and snow today. Sometimes we
may intend to rule out its being possible that both disjuncts of a true disjunction are true. For example, the father
who says 'We will go on a picnic or we will go to a movie'
may intend to rule out doing both. Using our present connectives, we could make such an intention explicit by using
a sentence having the form:

$$[(\Phi \ v \ \Psi) \ \& \sim (\Phi \ \& \ \Psi)].$$

[4] 'v' is also used to represent stylistic variants of 'or' such as 'either
. . . or . . .' and, usually, 'unless'.

In fact, the father in our example might well use a sentence of just this form to make his intention explicit; thus: 'Either we will go on a picnic or we will go to a movie, but not both'.

The next connective we will introduce is '→'. It will be useful, at least at first, to think of sentences having the form:

$$(\Phi \rightarrow \Psi)$$

as abbreviations for sentences having the form:

$$(\sim\Phi \lor \Psi).$$

The truth table for sentences of either form is the same:

Φ	Ψ	$\sim\Phi$	$(\sim\Phi \lor \Psi)$	$(\Phi \rightarrow \Psi)$
T	T	F	T	T
T	F	F	F	F
F	T	T	T	T
F	F	T	T	T

Further, by comparing this truth table with that given above for sentences of the form:

$$\sim(\Phi \ \& \ \sim\Psi)$$

we see that they also have the same truth conditions. Sentences having exactly the same truth conditions are said to be logically equivalent.

Our primary reason for introducing this new connective is that sentences of the form:

$$(\Phi \rightarrow \Psi)$$

reflect at least one important feature of English sentences of the form:

$$\text{If } \Phi, \text{ then } \Psi.$$

Such sentences—for example, 'If it is raining, then I will stay home'—are called conditional sentences. The sentence following 'If' (in this case, 'it is raining') is called the *antecedent*, while the sentence following 'then' (in this case, 'I will stay home') is called the *consequent*. The feature of such sentences reflected by sentences of the form:

$$(\Phi \rightarrow \Psi)$$

is that it is a basic part of the meaning of a conditional sentence that, if the antecedent is true and the consequent is false, then the entire conditional sentence is false. Thus, using the example above, if it is in fact raining, but I do not stay home, we would say that the statement 'If it is raining, then I will stay home' is false. We shall call any sentence of the form:

$$(\Phi \rightarrow \Psi)$$

a conditional sentence and use '$\rightarrow$' as a representation of the phrase 'if . . . , then . . .' as it occurs in sentences of the form:

$$\text{If } \Phi, \text{ then } \Psi.[5]$$

We do *not* take '$\rightarrow$' to be an abbreviation of 'implies'. We take implication to be a relation that holds between a

---

[5] There are a great many stylistic variants of the English phrase 'if . . . , then . . .'. Following is a partial list:

If Φ, then Ψ	Given that Φ, Ψ
Φ only if Ψ	Only if Ψ, Φ
Ψ if Φ	Ψ provided that Φ
Ψ in case Φ	Ψ assuming that Φ
Ψ on the condition that Φ	

We shall use sentences of the form $(\Phi \rightarrow \Psi)$ to abbreviate any of these stylistic variants.

sentence Φ and a sentence Ψ if Ψ is a logical consequence of Φ. Two specific examples will be helpful:

(1) If the horse's leg is broken, then the horse will be shot.
(2) 'The horse's leg is broken' implies 'The horse will be shot'.

Note that because (2) expresses a relationship (implication) between sentences, it contains two sentence names which have been formed by putting the sentences that they name within single quote marks. (Cf. VIII, 3.)[6] On the other hand (1), which does *not* express a relationship between sentences, does not contain any names of sentences. The first sentence may very well be true, but the second is not. For 'The horse will be shot' is not a logical consequence of 'The horse's leg is broken'.

Notice that it would be incorrect to interpret the truth table for conditionals as a truth table for implication even if we disregard the fact that 'implies' requires names of sentences, not sentences, on each side of it in order to produce a sentence. The difficulty is this: We would have to say that every sentence implies each true sentence and that each false sentence implies every sentence. (Consider lines 1, 3, and 4 of the truth table.) Consequently we shall treat 'implies' as expressing a relation between sentences, not as a phrase of connection enabling us to produce more complex sentences from simpler sentences, i.e., not as a sentential connective. (Cf. III, 1, A.)

Someone may well feel that it is also incorrect to sup-

[6] (Chapter VIII, Section 3.) This method of referring to other portions of the book will be used throughout.

pose that it is true that if Plato was a Greek, then General Motors produces Chevrolets. And surely the truth table for conditionals does commit us to this. (Consider line 1.) But we must be very cautious here. It is very unusual to find conditional sentences the antecedent and the consequent of which are about totally unrelated things. But once we recognize that such conditionals are possible, we find that it would be as peculiar to say that 'If Plato was a Greek, then General Motors produces Chevrolets' is false as it is to say that it is true. The oddity, then, arises not from considering such sentences to be true; rather, it arises from considering them at all.

An even more serious conflict with our initial intuitions arises when we consider the following conditional sentences and refer to lines 3 and 4 of the truth table for conditionals:

   (i) If Dionysius was born in 335 B.C., then Dionysius was born before 335 B.C.

  (ii) If Dionysius was born in 335 B.C., then Dionysius was not born in 1950.

 (iii) If Dionysius was born in 335 B.C., then Dionysius was born before 334 B.C.

 (iv) If Dionysius was born in 335 B.C., then Dionysius was born in 330 B.C.

Now assuming that Dionysius was born in 330 B.C., sentences (i)–(iv) all have false antecedents, and sentences (ii) and (iv) have true consequents. According to the truth table for conditionals, all four sentences are true since all have false antecedents. Yet most speakers of English would initially take only (ii) and (iii) to be true. We can represent this discrepancy as follows:

According to the truth table for '→', sentences (i)–(iv) would be true as follows:	According to our intuitive understanding of conditionals:
A (i) F → F : T	B (i) is F
(ii) F → T : T	(ii) is T
(iii) F → F : T	(iii) is T
(iv) F → T : T	(iv) is F

This shows that the truth table for sentences of the form:

$$(\Phi \rightarrow \Psi)$$

does not adequately reflect *all* our intuitions about conditional sentences in English. Moreover, it shows that no connective whose meaning could be given by means of a truth table could possibly capture *all* our initial intuitions about conditionals. For (i) and (iii) would both be represented by the same row of any truth table, as would (ii) and (iv). Yet according to our initial intuitions, (i) and (iii) differ in truth value, as do (ii) and (iv). We shall nonetheless use the truth table given for conditionals, bearing in mind these difficulties and remembering that sometimes—after thorough reflection—we come to give up our initial intuitions.

Finally we introduce the connective '↔' as a representation of 'if and only if'.[7] Sentences having the logical form:

$$(\Phi \leftrightarrow \Psi)$$

are called biconditionals. The reason for this characterization becomes obvious when we note that the truth conditions for biconditionals are the same as those for sentences of the form:

[7] '↔' is also used to represent stylistic variations of 'if and only if', such as 'exactly on the condition that' and, sometimes, 'just in case'.

$$[(\Phi \rightarrow \Psi) \,\&\, (\Psi \rightarrow \Phi)]$$

Φ	Ψ	$(\Phi \leftrightarrow \Psi)$	$(\Phi \rightarrow \Psi)$	$(\Psi \rightarrow \Phi)$	$[(\Phi \rightarrow \Psi) \,\&\, (\Psi \rightarrow \Phi)]$
T	T	T	T	T	T
T	F	F	F	T	F
F	T	F	T	F	F
F	F	T	T	T	T

To review, we have five connectives:[8]

not	~
and	&
or	v
if . . . , then . . .	→
. . . if and only if . . .	↔

Now consider the symbolization of some simple sentences:[9]

If you come, I won't drive.

P: You come.

Q: I will drive.

$$(P \rightarrow \sim Q)$$

---

[8] The following table indicates some alternative symbolizations in common use. Instead of:

~P:	$\overline{P}$, $\not\!P$, $-P$,			or NP
(P & Q):	(P • Q),	(P v Q),	(PQ),	or KPQ
(P v Q):				or APG
(P→Q):	(P⊃Q)			or CPQ
(P↔Q):	(P≡Q)			or EPQ

The last column is Polish notation, which eliminates the need for parentheses by a conventional ordering of symbols.

[9] Expressions like "P: You come" will be used in place of the more cumbersome: "Let 'P' abbreviate the sentence 'You come'."

If taxes are lowered and labor doesn't strike,
then and only then will prices drop.
  P: Taxes are lowered.
  Q: Labor strikes.
  R: Prices will drop.

$$[(P \& \sim Q) \leftrightarrow R]$$

P: It is raining.
It is raining and it is not raining.
  $(P \& \sim P)$
It is raining or it is not raining.
  $(P \vee \sim P)$

Compare the truth tables for sentences having the same
forms as these last two sentences:

Φ	$\sim\Phi$	$(\Phi \& \sim\Phi)$	$(\Phi \vee \sim\Phi)$
T	F	F	T
F	T	F	T

Sentences having the form:

$$(\Phi \& \sim\Phi)$$

are said to be contradictions. And sentences having the
form:

$$(\Phi \vee \sim\Phi)$$

are said to be tautologies. More generally, any sentence
whose *form* is such that a truth table for sentences of that
form reveals that the sentence is always false is said to be
a contradiction and is *logically* false. And any sentence
whose *form* is such that a truth table for sentences of that

form reveals that the sentence is always true is said to be a tautology and is *logically* true. Of course, not all false sentences are contradictions, nor are all true sentences tautologies.

The concepts of a logically false sentence and a logically true sentence are broader than the concepts of a contradiction and a tautology as defined here. That is, all contradictions are logically false, but not all logically false sentences are contradictions. Similarly, all tautologies are logically true, but not all logically true sentences are tautologies. For example, 'Some red thing is not red' is logically false; but no truth table will reveal that it is always false. And 'All brothers are brothers' is logically true, but no truth table will reveal that it is always true.

We may now introduce the notion of *consistency*. We say that a set of sentences is consistent if it is possible that all the sentences in the set are true. Thus the set:

(1) $(P \rightarrow Q)$
(2) $(R \rightarrow \sim Q)$
(3) P
(4) R

is an *inconsistent* set. Consider the truth-table for conditionals and that for conjunctions. According to the truth table for conditionals, if (1) and (3) are true, then it is true that Q; and if (2) and (4) are true, then it is true that $\sim Q$. But according to the truth table for conjunction, if it is true that Q and it is true that $\sim Q$, then it is true that $(Q \& \sim Q)$. But we have seen that it is not possible for any sentence having the form:

$$(\Phi \& \sim \Phi)$$

to be true. So it is not possible for all the sentences in this set to be true; therefore the set that consists of sentences (1), (2), (3), and (4) is inconsistent.

Finally, consider again the sentence 'All brothers are brothers'. This sentence, although logically true, has no sentential connectives. Thus, the only truth table possible for this sentence is that for sentences having the form Φ. And this truth table is:

$$
\begin{array}{c}
\Phi \\
\hline\hline
T \\
\hline
F
\end{array}
$$

Whether or not a sentence is logically true depends on its logical form. Such a table, obviously, does not reveal the logical form in virtue of which 'All brothers are brothers' is logically true. To exhibit the logical form of such sentences, we need a much more powerful set of techniques. A small part of these techniques will be considered in the next chapter.

Exercises

1. What does it mean to say of an argument that it is sound? valid? Illustrate the difference with examples.

2. Each argument can be represented by a profile that indicates the truth value of each line in the argument and also the validity and soundness of the argument. For example, in:

> P₁ All people breathe.
> P₂ Jones is a person.
> C   Jones breathes.

the premises and conclusion are true, and the argument

is valid and sound. We can therefore write its profile as:

T
T
T
V
S.

On the other hand:

P₃ All men are mortal.
P₄ Fish live in trees.
C Birds fly.

has a profile of:

T
F
T
I
U.

Whereas a profile can be written for each argument, it is not the case that an argument can be found to correspond to each profile. For instance, no argument can have:

T
T
F
V
S

T
T

as its profile, because F is incompatible with V (which

means the conclusion cannot be false if the premises are true).

Write down every possible profile for arguments with two premises, and for each one either give an example of an argument that clearly has that profile or else explain in detail exactly why no such argument can be found.

3. If the conclusion of a valid argument is a logically false sentence, what can we say about the truth values of the premises of that argument?

4. Is $[\sim(P \& Q) \leftrightarrow (\sim P \text{ v } Q)]$ a tautology, a contradiction, or neither? Justify your answer by constructing a truth table.

5. Give an example to show that not only tautologies are true.

6. Is $(\sim P \rightarrow Q)$ equivalent to $(P \text{ v } Q)$? Prove with truth tables that your answer is correct.

7. A. Symbolize the following sentences using 'P_1' for 'The sun shines' and 'P_2' for 'I'll be at the beach':
  (a) If the sun shines, I'll be at the beach.
  (b) I'll be at the beach unless the sun doesn't shine
  (c) Either the sun doesn't shine or I'll be at the beach (or perhaps both).
  (d) It is not the case that both the sun shines and I'll not be at the beach.

B. From the truth tables that give the truth conditions for sentences (a) through (d), what can we say about the logical relations (consistency, logical equivalence, and implication) among these four sentences?

8. Symbolize the following sentences, indicating the abbreviations you are using for each sentence:
    (a) You read with care or you learn little.
    (b) If there is smoke, there is fire.
    (c) I will go if the sun shines, otherwise not.
    (d) All scholars ruminate.
    (e) Johnny may have cake or ice cream, but not both.

9. Express the exclusive sense of disjunction in terms of '~', '&', and 'v', and show by a truth table that your expression is correct.

II

Predicate Calculus and Sets

1. Predicate Calculus

The concepts and symbols introduced thus far do not allow us to exhibit the logical form of such sentences as 'All brothers are male siblings'. The general claim exemplified by this sentence is that all things having a certain property (that of being a brother, in this case) also have another property (that of being a male sibling). To symbolize such a sentence merely as 'P' leaves the details of its internal structure inexplicit, and it is often this structure that determines the role of the sentence in arguments.

In what follows, the concepts and techniques for exhibiting the logical form of simple sentences will be developed, so that we will have a more powerful method for the analysis of sentences and arguments.

As an example of an obviously valid argument, consider:

> All Athenians are wise.
> <u>Callias is an Athenian.</u>
> Callias is wise.

A. As a first step in symbolizing this argument, we abbreviate the name 'Callias' with 'c'. We shall use lower-class letters (with or without subscripts, but excluding 'x', 'y', and 'z') to denote particular individuals; such terms are called *individual constants*. We use constants to abbreviate not only proper names such as 'Callias' but also definite descriptions such as 'the wisest man in Athens'. We may, for example, let the constant 'd' abbreviate the phrase 'the wisest man in Athens'.

B. The sentence 'Callias is wise' consists of a subject ('Callias') and a *predicate* ('is wise'). We shall abbreviate predicates by capital letters (with or without subscripts).[1] In this case, let us replace 'is wise' by the *predicate symbol* 'W'. We shall adopt the convention of writing the constant abbreviating the subject of predication immediately after the predicate symbol, so that 'Callias is wise' will be symbolized by 'Wc'.

It is often true that a particular sentence can be symbolized in several different ways. As an example, consider:

Callias is wise and Callias is an Athenian.

This sentence can be symbolized in at least two ways:

(a) On the basis of the scheme of abbreviation:
    W: is wise
    A: is an Athenian
    c: Callias
    (Wc & Ac).
(b) On the basis of the scheme of abbreviation:
    B: is wise and is an Athenian
    c: Callias
    Bc.

---

[1] We except 'P', 'Q', and 'R', which are reserved for abbreviation of sentences. (Cf. I, 3.)

Which of these symbolizations of the original sentence is chosen will depend on the context in which it is to be used.

The predicate 'is wise' is a *one-place* predicate because the result of writing the predicate symbol that abbreviates it followed by one individual constant is a sentence. Some predicates are two-place—for example, 'loves'. 'John loves Mary' may be symbolized by 'Ljm' on the basis of the scheme of abbreviation:

$$L(1)(2): (1) \text{ loves } (2).^2$$
$$j: \text{John}$$
$$m: \text{Mary}.$$

And, of course, there are higher-place predicates, such as 'lies between' in the sentence 'Point a lies between points b and f, symbolized by 'Babf' on the basis of:

$$B(1)(2)(3): (1) \text{ lies between } (2) \text{ and } (3)$$
$$a: \text{point } a$$
$$b: \text{point } b$$
$$f: \text{point } f.$$

Note that verbs are not the only words that can be symbolized by predicate symbols (as the word 'predicate' may lead one to expect). Adverbs, adjectives, and prepositional phrases may all be symbolized by predicate symbols. Consider, as an example, the sentence 'Callias talks in the Academy with Plato'. We can treat everything after the word 'Callias' as a predicate and symbolize the sentence by 'Tc' on the basis of the scheme of abbreviation:

---

[2] Notice that 'John loves Mary' and 'Mary loves John' are different sentences, although each is composed of the same predicate and names. In general, the order of individual constants following a two or more place predicate symbol must be indicated in the scheme of abbreviation. We shall also indicate the subject position for one-place predicates.

T (1): (1) talks in the Academy with Plato
    c: Callias:

On the other hand, we may treat the predicate as a two-place predicate, symbolizing the sentence by 'T₁cp' on the basis of the scheme:

T$_1$ (1) (2): (1) talks in the Academy with (2)
    c: Callias
    p: Plato.

In general, a one-place predicate may be constructed from a two-place predicate by filling one of the places in the latter with a name or definite description (as 'Plato' was added to the predicate 'talks in the Academy with' to form the one-place predicate 'talks in the Academy with Plato').

C. Consider the symbolization of the following sentences:

Callias is wise.   Wc
Socrates is wise.   Ws
Aristophanes is wise.   Wa

The form or pattern common to these expressions may be indicated by introducing *individual variables* such as 'x' in the expression 'Wx'. (We shall use 'x', 'y', and 'z', with or without subscripts, for variables.) Such variables do not denote any particular individual.

D. In addition, a variable may be thought of as corresponding roughly to a pronoun in ordinary language. Since Callias is wise, we may truly say:

(1) There exists someone, such that he is wise.

In symbolizing (1), we must make use of a variable, since the 'he' in (1) does not refer to any specified person, only to *someone*. Therefore, we begin the symbolization of (1) as follows:

(1a) There exists an x such that x is wise.

(1b) There exists an x such that Wx.

Finally, we introduce the *quantifier* '(∃x)' to stand for 'There exists an x':

(1c) (∃x) Wx.

(Note the use of parentheses to set off the quantifier from the rest of the sentence.)

Of course, it makes no difference which variable we use; (1) could just as well have been translated by '(∃y) Wy'.

The quantifier '(∃x)' is also read as 'for some x' or 'there is at least one x'.

Next, consider the sentence:

(2) Everything in the universe is green. That is,

(2a) Each thing x is such that it is green. Or,

(2b) Each thing x is such that x is green.

We introduce the quantifier '(x)' for 'Each thing x is such that'. Then on the basis of the scheme of abbreviation:

$$G (1): (1) \text{ is green.}$$

(2) may be symbolized by:

(2c) (x) Gx.

(Here again 'y' could have been used in place of 'x'.)

The quantifier (∃x) is called the *existential* quantifier; (x) is called the *universal* quantifier.[3]

---

[3] Some other symbols used for quantifiers are:
Instead of:

(∃x)	(Ex), Vx
(x)	(∀x), ∧x

E. Following are some examples of the translation of English sentences into the symbolic logic notation just introduced. The following scheme of abbreviation is adopted for these examples:

A(1):   (1) is an Athenian
C(1):   (1) is a Cretan
W(1):   (1) is wise
S(1) (2):   (1) is smarter than (2).

(1) All Athenians are wise.

That is:

(1a) Each thing is such that if it is an Athenian, then it is wise.
(1b) (x) (Ax → Wx).

One may be tempted to translate (1) by:

(1c) (x) (Ax & Wx).

But (1c) is clearly incorrect, for its English translation is 'All things are Athenians and are wise', which has not at all the same meaning as (1).

(2)   Some Athenians are wise.
(2a) There is at least one thing such that it is an Athenian and it is wise.
(2b) ($\exists x$) (Ax & Wx).

In the case of this second example, it would be *incorrect* to write:

(2c) ($\exists x$) (Ax → Wx),

because (2) is true only if there exists at least one wise Athenian, whereas (2c) may be true even if there are *no* wise Athenians. This can be seen by referring back to the truth table for conditionals and noting that expressions having the form:

$$(\Phi \rightarrow \Psi)$$

have the same truth table as expressions having the form:

$$(\sim\!\Phi \ \mathrm{v} \ \Psi).$$

Thus, '$(Ax \rightarrow Wx)$' and '$(\sim\!Ax \ \mathrm{v} \ Wx)$' are equivalent; therefore we may replace (2c) by:

(2d) $(\exists x) \ (\sim\!Ax \ \mathrm{v} \ Wx).$

But (2d) means that there exists something which is either *not* an Athenian or which *is* wise, so that (2d) is true so long as there is at least one thing which is not an Athenian. Thus, (2d), which is equivalent to (2c), can be true even when there are *no* wise Athenians, and it is clear that (2c) is not the correct translation of (2).

> (3) Athenians are smarter than Cretans.
> (3a) Each thing x and each thing y are such that if x is an Athenian and y is a Cretan, then x is smarter than y.
> (3b) $(x) \ (y) \ ((Ax \ \& \ Cy) \rightarrow Sxy).$

The third example illustrates the use of more than one quantifier:

> (4) Some Athenians are not wise.

This sentence may be symbolized in two ways. First consider it as a denial of (1):

> (4a) It is not the case that all Athenians are wise.
> (4b) $\sim\!(x) \ (Ax \rightarrow Wx).$

Or we can paraphrase (4) by:

> (4c) There is at least one thing such that it is an Athenian and it is not wise.
>
> (4d) $(\exists x)(Ax \,\&\, \sim Wx)$.

Actually, it can be shown that (4b) and (4d) are equivalent in the sense that each follows logically from the other.

F. Finally, we shall symbolize the argument with which this section began:

> (I) All Athenians are wise.
>   Callias is an Athenian.
>   (therefore) Callias is wise.
>
> (Ia) $(x)(Ax \rightarrow Wx)$
>   Ac
>   ∴ Wc.

The argument is clearly valid, because if it is true of all individuals that, if they are Athenians, then they are wise, then it is certainly true of any particular individual, say c, that if c is an Athenian, he is wise. The second premise tells us that c is indeed an Athenian. Therefore, c is wise.

But not all arguments are so transparent, and it is necessary to specify exactly and in detail what sort of inferences can be made legitimately. This is done by means of a set of rules usually called rules of inference. One common rule of inference would allow us to infer 'Ha' from '$(x)Hx$'. It would also allow the inference of '$(y)((Ac \,\&\, Cy) \rightarrow Scy)$' from (3b). That is, we could infer from (3b) that each thing y is such that if Callias is an Athenian and y is a Cretan, then Callias is smarter than y.

To specify an adequate set of rules is too lengthy a task to be undertaken here. The important points to note about rules of inference are the following: Following these rules allows us to infer from a set of sentences (premises) another sentence (a conclusion), with the guarantee that if the premises are true, the conclusion cannot be false. That is, if an argument is constructed so that the conclusion follows according to the rules of inference, we are assured that the argument is valid. Specifying the rules of inference gives content to the phrase 'follows logically'. To assert that a sentence Ψ follows logically from a sentence Φ is to assert that a string of sentences can be exhibited, beginning with Φ and ending with Ψ, such that each member of the string follows from one or more of the preceding members according to a rule of inference.

We are now in a position to state, very briefly, part of what is involved in constructing a predicate calculus.

To establish such a system of symbolic notation, we must first specify a vocabulary and give the rules for constructing sentences using this vocabulary. This involves listing those symbols that can be used as individual constants, one-place predicate symbols, two-place predicate symbols, and so on. Then rules are devised that state which strings of symbols are to be allowed as *well formed*—that is, which are of a form that makes sense (such as 'Wc') and which are not (such as 'cꓱW'). Second, the rules of inference are given. As noted above, they specify how one sentence can be inferred from another sentence or set of sentences.

It is important to note that these rules may be specified without any reference to the notion of truth or to English words for which the symbols stand. That is, we may consider how a sentence such as Wc can be combined with other sentences, what its role is in various arguments, and whether or not it is well formed, without considering it as standing for some English sentence and without considering its truth or falsity.

Such rules are called *syntactical*. Syntax is the study of the forms of certain groups of symbols abstracted from any questions about their content. In the preceding sections, we have closely related our remarks about logic to the English language—even introducing the symbols '&' and 'v' to represent 'and' and 'or'—because the important use of logic for our purposes is in symbolizing English sentences and determining the validity of arguments. But it should be emphasized that logic proper is independent of any particular natural language.

This should not be taken to suggest that logic is concerned only with syntax. Systems of deductive logic are developed with constant attention to the goals of preserving truth and not introducing information into the conclusion that is not contained in the premises of an argument. Further, connectives are not just meaningless marks; for example, '&' is given a meaning by the truth table for conjunction. Logic may be usefully thought of as the study of syntactical devices for capturing concepts such as truth and validity. These concepts, among others, which are related to questions of meaning, are called *semantic* concepts. (Cf. IX, 5 and 8.)

Often a formal system of logic is used to study a particular language or segment of language. In that case we must specify, in addition to the above rules, certain informal rules of translation from the formal language to the natural language. (For example, in English one must specify that 'W' stands for 'is wise'.) And further, we must specify what entities the variables range over and what the constants denote.

Once we have made these rules, we have at our disposal a very powerful tool for the analysis of languages, arguments, and concepts.

2. Sets

The notion of a set is, intuitively, the notion of a collection of things of one sort or another. Words often used synonymously with 'set' are 'class' and 'collection'. Examples of sets are:

> the set of all wise men,
> the set of chessmen owned by Jones,
> the set of kangaroos over twenty feet tall,
> the set of all positive odd integers,
> the set of letters in the Greek alphabet.

The examples illustrate that sets may have a finite or an infinite number of members and that the members may be concrete physical objects or abstract entities like numbers. Note that even though the members of a particular set may be physical objects, the set itself is not another physical object but an abstract entity. Note also that a set may be empty; that is, it may have *no* members. Such is (as far as we know) the set of kangaroos over twenty feet tall.

The Greek letter 'ϵ' is used to represent 'is a member of'. Therefore, '$a\epsilon B$' is to be read 'a is a member of (the set) B'.

If we wish to enumerate specifically the members of a set, we enclose the names of its members in braces; thus, '$\{1,2,3\}$' names the set composed of the integers 1, 2, and 3. If $B = \{1,2,3\}$, it is true that $1 \epsilon B$. The number 4, however, does not belong to B; and this may be indicated by writing '$4 \notin B$'—i.e., '$\notin$' represents 'does not belong to'.

We can employ some of the symbols and concepts of predicate calculus by observing that there is a close connection between sets and properties. An object has a certain

property if, and only if, the object is a member of the set
of objects having that property. The set of all Athenians
can, therefore, be characterized as the set of all x such that
x is an Athenian (Ax). Call this set '⊙'; we write:

$$\Theta = \{x|Ax\}.$$

(Here '{x|Ax}' is read 'the set of all x such that x is an
Athenian'.) We know that c∈⊙ (where c, as above, denotes
Callias).

Many sentences that can be translated into the notation
of predicate logic can be equally well symbolized using the
notation of set theory. 'All Athenians are wise' may be
written, for example:

$$(1) \quad (x) \quad (x \in \Theta \rightarrow x \in \Omega),$$

where ⊙ = {x|Ax} and Ω = {x|Wx}. A partial English trans-
lation of (1) is:

For all x, if x belongs to the set of Athenians, then x
belongs also to the set of those who are wise (where 'x'
ranges over human beings).

Two sets, A and B, are identical if and only if they have
exactly the same members. Symbolically:

$$A = B \leftrightarrow (x) \ (x \in A \leftrightarrow x \in B).$$

In a trivial sense, A is identical to A, since it is obviously
true that:

$$(x) \ (x \in A \leftrightarrow x \in A).$$

We speak of a set A as being a *subset* of another set B
when every member of A is also a member of B. We use
the symbol '⊆' for 'is a subset of'. Symbolically:

$$A \subseteq B \leftrightarrow (x) \ (x \in A \rightarrow x \in B).$$

Thus, $\{1,2,3\}$ is a subset of $\{1,2,3,4\}$, but the converse is not the case. In a trivial sense, any set A is a subset of itself, since for any set A it will be true that:

$$(x) \ (x \epsilon A \rightarrow x \epsilon A).$$

Thus $\{1,4,7\}$ is a subset of $\{1,4,7\}$. We now introduce the notion of a *proper subset*, so as to distinguish between those subsets of a given set A that are not equivalent to A, and A itself. We introduce the symbol '$\subset$' for 'is a proper subset of'. Thus:

$$A \subset B \leftrightarrow [(x) \ (x \epsilon A \rightarrow x \epsilon B) \ \& \sim (x) \ (x \epsilon B \rightarrow x \epsilon A)].$$

We may say, for example, that the set of husbands is a proper subset of the set of men and is equivalent to the set of married men.

As mentioned above, a set may be empty—i.e., have no members. Then, trivially, if sets θ and Ω are empty, they have the same members and hence are not two sets, but one (i.e., $\theta = \Omega$). Therefore there is just one empty set and it is called the *null set*. It is usually designated by 'Λ' and is characterized as follows:

$$\Lambda = \{x \mid x \neq x\}.$$

Since there is no object x that is not identical with itself, nothing satisfies the condition $x \neq x$; and the set Λ is empty (null).

Since every object satisfies the condition $x = x$, we can characterize the *universal set* 'V', which contains everything:

$$V = \{x \mid x = x\}.$$

Sometimes two different sets have some elements in common. For example, $\{1,2,3,4,6\}$ and $\{2,4,5\}$ have 2 and 4 in common. The set {2,4} of common elements is called the *intersection* of the two original sets. The intersection of θ and Ω is designated θ ∩ Ω and is characterized as follows:

$$\theta \cap \Omega = \{x \mid (x \in \theta \,\&\, x \in \Omega)\ \}.$$

Sometimes we are interested in all the elements that are in either of two sets. In the above example, those elements are 1, 2, 3, 4, 5, and 6. The set containing them is called the *union* of the two original sets. The union of sets θ and Ω is designated θ ∪ Ω and is characterized as follows:

$$\theta \cup \Omega = \{x \mid (x \in \theta \ v \ x \in \Omega)\ \}.$$

Now let us reconsider the universal set, introduced above. This reconsideration will lead us to one of the most striking discoveries in modern logic. If V contains *everything*, then it contains itself. A few other sets have this peculiar feature of being members of themselves, for instance, the set of all sets. Formally, a set θ has this peculiar feature if and only if θ ∈ θ. Let us consider all those sets which do *not* have this feature, that is, all those sets that are not elements of themselves. For example, {1,2,3} is not a member of itself. Such sets satisfy the condition: θ ∉ θ. And the set R of all such sets may be characterized:

$$R = \{\theta \mid \theta \notin \theta\}.$$

In other words, R is the set of all those sets which satisfy the condition θ ∉ θ, that is, those sets which do not contain themselves as members. Now consider: Does R contain itself? Assume it does. Then R ∈ R. Therefore R does not satisfy the condition θ ∉ θ and hence is not in R. In other words, R does not contain itself, contrary to the assumption. We must reject the assumption if it leads to its own denial. Let us then assume instead that R does not contain itself. Then R ∉ R; and R satisfies the condition θ ∉ θ and is therefore a member of the set of all sets which satisfy that condition. In other words, R ∈ R, contrary to assumption. This paradox was discovered by Bertrand Russell and is known as Russell's paradox. It has profound importance for logic and the foundations of mathematics. It also serves as a dramatic illustration of the point that what seems simple and clear on the surface is often agonizingly difficult to understand on closer and more sophisticated examination. In this instance, it seemed easy enough to talk about the set of all sets that do not contain themselves. Yet that idea leads to paradox, and we can no longer be so confident in our ability to understand what seems to be a straightforward description of a set.

Exercises

1. Find an example of a deductive argument in a newspaper, magazine, or textbook and indicate the premises and conclusion.

2. Symbolize the following sentences, providing a scheme of abbreviation for each:
   a. If John is tall, then either Smith is shorter than Dokes or the coach is mistaken.
   b. Joe goes just in case the sun shines.
   c. The vice-chairman goes just in case the chairman is absent.
   d. Every philosopher thinks about some problem.
   e. No one is at home.
   f. All logicians are acute or I have been misled.

3. Is it reasonable to infer 'Ma' from '(x) (Hx → Mx)' and 'Ha'? Why?

4. On the basis of the scheme of abbreviation:

L (*1*) (*2*): (*1*) is larger than (*2*),

(x) (y) Lxy: Everything is larger than everything.

(∃x) (y) Lxy: Something is larger than everything.

Exercise. Translate the following sentences into English:

    a. (x) (∃y) Lxy
    b. (x) (∃y) Lyx
    c. (x) (y) Lyx
    d. (∃x) (y) Lyx
    e. (∃x) (∃y) Lxy
    f. (∃x) (∃y) Lyx
    g. (∃y) (∃x) Lxy
    h. (∃y) (∃x) Lyx.

5. A = {1,2,4,3}
  B = {1,2,3,4}
  Are A and B identical?

6. List all the subsets of {1,2,3}.

7. Explain briefly why it must be the case that:

    a. (Ω) (Λ ⊆ Ω)
    b. (Ω) (Ω ⊆ V)

III

Further Logical Notions

1. *Important Terms*

What follows are some remarks about the meanings and uses of a few key words and phrases which occur sufficiently often in philosophical writings to deserve special attention. These words are discussed here because, although they are often used outside the context of logic, they constitute an important part of the technical vocabulary of logical analysis.

A. 'IMPLY', 'INFER', AND 'ENTAIL'

These are three closely related words that can easily be misused. Roughly, the distinction between the first two is that *people* infer whereas *sentences* imply. If Φ and Ψ are sentences, we may say:

(1) Jones infers Ψ from Φ.
(2) Sentence Φ implies sentence Ψ.

(1) means in part that Jones considers it to be the case that Ψ is a consequence of Φ. But Jones can be in error; he can infer incorrectly. In contrast, Φ cannot incorrectly imply Ψ—either Ψ is a logical consequence of Φ or it is not; and

to say that Φ implies Ψ is simply to say that Ψ is a logical consequence of Φ. Thus, the phrase 'incorrectly implies' has no correct use.

We may characterize inference, therefore, as a relation between a *person* and two sets of sentences (premises and conclusion); to infer is to accept a conclusion on the basis of a set of premises—if one accepts the premises. ('Infer' is sometimes used in a derivative sense to mean 'conclude from the *fact* that . . .' instead of 'conclude from the *premises* that . . .'.) Examples:

(3) Jones inferred from the first three premises that a does not equal b.

(4) Jones inferred from the fact that the sun was up that it was later than 5 A.M.

Implication, on the other hand, strictly construed, is a relation between two sets of sentences. Consider:

(5) 'All Athenians are wise and Callias is an Athenian' implies 'Callias is wise'.

'Imply' is also used in a derivative sense as a relation among *facts*. Thus:

(6) The fact that Callias is an Athenian and all Athenians are wise implies the fact that Callias is wise.

Unfortunately, the picture is a little more complicated than has yet been indicated, because there is a use of 'imply' in which *people* are said to imply.

(7) The speaker implied that war was imminent.

We make take (7) to be short for 'The speaker implied *by what he said* that war was imminent'. But even if we construe (7) to mean that it was the sentences used by the speaker rather than the speaker himself that implied the imminence of war, there is one further notable difference in the way 'imply' is used in (7). When we say that a person implied something, we don't always mean that what is implied is a logical consequence of what he said; sometimes we mean that, in saying what he said, he suggested or hinted at some conclusion. In this sense, 'imply' has a meaning close to that of 'intimate'.

Reason was given on page 16 against supposing that the truth table for conditionals gives the meaning of 'implies'. Neither does that truth table give the meaning of 'entails'. We shall henceforth use 'entail' as a synonym of 'imply', in that sense in which sentences, not people, imply. Thus we shall take the assertion that a sentence Φ entails a sentence Ψ to mean that Ψ is a logical consequence of Φ.

B. 'PRESUPPOSE' AND PRESUPPOSITIONS

Although the expression 'presuppose' is sometimes (perhaps misleadingly) used in much the same way as 'imply', in the clearest use of the expression it is *people* who presuppose. In this sense, 'presuppose' means to assume or to take for granted the truth of some sentence without explicitly acknowledging or recognizing that fact. Examples:

(1) When Smith argued that the senses provide us with accurate information about external physical objects, he was presupposing that such objects exist.

(2) Most ancient Greek astronomers presupposed that all heavenly bodies moved in circular paths.

It is part of the philosopher's task to make as many of his presuppositions as explicit as is feasible; sometimes those things taken most for granted are most in need of careful inspection.

This process of making presuppositions explicit cannot go on without limit, of course. No one expects a physicist to include reasons for supposing that the sun exists, in a paper on nuclear processes in the sun's corona, even though the scientist does presuppose that the sun exists.

C. CONTRADICTION AND CONSISTENCY

Two sentences are *contradictory* if and only if one is the negation of the other or is logically equivalent to the negation of the other. Thus, 'It is raining' and 'It is not the case that it is raining' are contradictory sentences. Their conjunction, 'It is raining and it is not raining', is a *contradiction.*

The term 'consistent' is predicated of sets of sentences. A set of sentences is *consistent* if and only if no contradiction is a logical consequence of the sentences in the set. Two sentences are *consistent with* each other if there is a consistent set of which they are members. The *set* of sentences consisting of 'Callias is wise' and 'Socrates is an Athenian' is consistent. And the *sentences* 'Callias is wise' and 'Socrates is an Athenian' are consistent with each other. The set consisting of the sentences 'All Athenians are wise', 'Callias is an Athenian', and 'Callias is not wise' is *inconsistent* because the contradiction 'Callias is wise and Callias is not wise' is a logical consequence of the set. Two sentences are *inconsistent* with each other if *every* set of which they are members is inconsistent.

D. NECESSARY AND SUFFICIENT CONDITIONS

(1) If Carl won the two-mile race, then Carl officially entered the two-mile race.

(2) If Carl, and only Carl, ran the two-mile race in the

fastest time ever recorded, then Carl won the two-mile race.

These two sentences are chosen to illustrate the difference between *necessary* and *sufficient* conditions. The truth of 'Carl officially entered the two-mile race' is a necessary condition for the truth of 'Carl won the two-mile race'; that is, it is necessary to enter a race in order to win it. But clearly, it is not sufficient for winning a race that one enter it. Something more is required—namely, officially completing the course before any other contestant.

Consider (2). The truth of 'Carl, and only Carl, ran the two-mile race in the fastest time ever recorded' is a sufficient condition for the truth of 'Carl won the two-mile race'; that is, it is sufficient to win a race that one run the race in the fastest recorded time and be the only one to do so. But it is not necessary, because it is possible to win a particular race and still not break any record.

When two sentences are connected by 'If . . . , then . . .', the first sentence is called the antecedent and the second the consequent. We may generalize the remarks made about the example sentences by saying that the truth of the antecedent of a true conditional sentence is a sufficient condition for the truth of the consequent. The truth of the consequent is, on the other hand, a necessary condition for the truth of the antecedent. Consider sentences (1) and (2) again. The truth of 'Carl won the two-mile race', which is the antecedent in sentence (1), is a sufficient condition for the truth of 'Carl officially entered the two-mile race', since no one can win a race in which he is not officially entered. And the truth of 'Carl won the two-mile race', which is the consequent in sentence (2), is a necessary condition for the truth of 'Carl, and only Carl, ran the two-mile race in the fastest time ever recorded', since he could not have run the race in the fastest recorded time, and have been the only one to do so, without winning. In a true biconditional sentence, '. . . if and only if . . .', the truth of either of the two sentences connected by 'if and only if' is a necessary *and* sufficient condition for the truth of the other. As an example, consider:

(3) Joel is Martha's husband if and only if Martha is Joel's wife.

E. 'IS' AND 'SAME'

1. The verb 'to be' is used in at least four ways, which should be carefully distinguished.

First, note that 'is' may be used to indicate identity. The sentence 'Callias is the wisest man in Athens' may be symbolized by 'c = d', where 'd' abbreviates 'the wisest man in Athens'. That is, Callias is identical with that wisest man. In the sentence 'Two plus two is four', 'is' again means the same as 'is identical with'.

Second, 'is' may be used to predicate some property of an object. The 'is' of predication is illustrated by 'Callias is wise'.[1]

Third, we sometimes use 'is' to indicate the unqualified existence of something as in the sentence 'He is' (i.e., 'he

---

[1] That the predicative use of the verb 'to be' is further complicated may be seen by considering the following examples:
(1) Condors are large.
(2) Condors are becoming extinct.
If we assume that both of these sentences exemplify the same predicative use of 'are', we must conclude that the properties of being large and of becoming extinct are attributed to different kinds of objects. For although an individual condor may be large, no individual condor can become extinct.

exists'). In this case no property is predicated of the subject; we are merely claiming that the subject exists.

Finally, 'is' may be used to indicate class inclusion. For example, 'Pleasure is good' may mean that the class of pleasant things is included in the class of good things. (Cf. II, 2.)

These distinctions are so straightforward that one may well wonder why they are made at all. The fact is that it is not always a simple matter to decide which way 'is' is being used, and it is sometimes easy to be misled by failing to make these distinctions. For example, the fact that 'is' can play these different roles can lead to confusion as to whether a particular statement is a factual claim or a definition. In fact, an example used above (i.e., 'Pleasure is good') may in some contexts be correctly interpreted as utilizing the 'is' of identity and in other contexts be correctly interpreted as utilizing the 'is' of predication. Occasionally a philosopher may not be clear himself as to which of these possible claims he wishes to assert. He may then use several different arguments, each of which would be support for a different claim, to support what appears to be one claim.

2. The word 'same' suffers from an ambiguity similar to that of 'is'.

Consider as an example the sentence 'This is the same card that I drew in the cut last night'. 'Same' here may indicate that there is only one card referred to, i.e., that the deck used last night is the deck being used now, and the card drawn last night is identical with the card now drawn. But 'same' could also indicate that the card drawn now is indistinguishable in respect to some specifiable (though in this case unspecified) criteria, e.g., rank and suit. The distinction being made here can be clarified by giving two different paraphrases, which utilize the notion of a set:

(1) The card I have now drawn is a member of all and only those sets of which the card I drew last night is a member.

(2) There is a set of card kinds (e.g., the set of fives of spades) of which both the card that I have now drawn and the card that I drew last night are members.

In using 'same' in this second sense, to indicate that two things belong to the same set, it must be clear what the relevant characteristics are in virtue of which the objects are said to belong to one set. The context of discussion will usually make this clear. For example, the claim that all brands of aspirin are the same would generally be taken to mean that in respect to such characteristics as relieving pain, reducing fever, and so forth, they are all about equally effective but not that they are alike in respect to retail price or annual advertising budget.

But it is often the case that it is not at all clear what is meant by a statement of the form 'A and B are the same' or 'A is like B'. This imprecision of 'same' and 'like' is emphasized in riddles such as the Mad Hatter's famous question, 'Why is a raven like a writing desk?' Unfortunately, some philosophical statements turn out to be riddles when they are not intended to be.

F. 'MUTUALLY EXCLUSIVE' AND 'JOINTLY EXHAUSTIVE'

The phrase 'mutually exclusive' expresses a relation that holds between any two sets just in case no member of either set is a member of the other. In an extended sense, the sets in a given collection of sets can be said to be *mutually exclusive* if and only if no two sets in the collection have any member in common. Thus, the set of even positive integers and the set of odd positive integers are mutually exclusive because there is nothing that belongs to both sets.

In any particular application of the concepts and techniques of set theory, we have in mind a collection of objects that can be members of the sets with which we are concerned. That is, if we are discussing real number theory, we will be interested in sets whose members are real numbers. Or we may be discussing sets whose members are men, factories, and so on. In each case, we can specify a *domain of discourse*—a collection of entities from which may be drawn the members of the particular sets under discussion. The sets in a given collection of sets are said to be *jointly exhaustive* (with respect to a specified domain of discourse) if and only if every member of the domain is a member of one or more of the sets in the collection.

If we take as the domain the set of positive integers, then the two sets of odd and even integers mentioned above are jointly exhaustive. If our domain is the set of positive real numbers, then those two sets are not jointly exhaustive, because the number π, for example, is a positive real number but not an integer.

The sets in a collection of sets may be jointly exhaustive without being mutually exclusive and vice versa.

As a final illustration, let the domain of discourse $\mathcal{D}$ be specified by:

$$\mathcal{D} = \{A,B,C,D,E\}$$

(1) The sets $\{A\}$, $\{B\}$, $\{C\}$, $\{D\}$, $\{E\}$, are mutually exclusive and jointly exhaustive.

(2) The sets {A,B}, {B,C}, {D,E} are jointly exhaustive but not mutually exclusive.

(3) The sets {A}, {B}, {C,D} are mutually exclusive but not jointly exhaustive.

We often speak loosely of properties rather than sets being mutually exclusive, meaning that no object can have both properties. For example, evenness and oddness (of numbers) are mutually exclusive properties.

G. UNIVERSALS AND PARTICULARS

The predicate calculus, as described above, rests on a distinction between referring expressions (such as individual constants and definite descriptions) and classificatory or characterizing expressions (such as predicates of varying complexity). This distinction is a reflection of a traditional philosophical distinction between *particulars* and *universals*.

Intuitively, a particular is any individual entity. Socrates, the number five, and the third manhole cover going east from Broadway on 42nd Street are each particulars.

Typically, our talk about particular entities consists in attributing some property to the individual in question. Thus, when we claim that the barn is red, we employ the predicate 'is red', which is (or might be) true of more than one individual. But the use of such general expressions poses the following question. How are we to account for the fact that individuals have *properties* (e.g., redness) in common, that they seem to share certain common *patterns* and *characteristics,* and that we can speak meaningfully of *kinds* of things? One traditional answer to this question is that, besides particulars, there exist also such common characteristics or properties; they are called *universals*.

Examples of universals are redness, tallness, honor, beauty, and evenness (as attributed to numbers). A universal may have many instances, one instance, or no instances; the concept of positive even prime number is a universal that has one instance; and the concept of unicorn is a universal that, as far as is known, has no instances. There will be a universal corresponding to each general expression, such as 'red', 'man', 'unicorn', or 'tall'. Universals, of course, are abstract entities that have no spatial extension and are not to be met in sense experience in the way that physical objects are.

The particular-universal distinction, then, is concerned with the question 'What exists?' and is separate from the grammatical distinction between singular and general terms, though closely related to it. Plato argued that universals exist and that their existence does not depend on the existence of particulars. Other philosophers have denied that universals exist while still seeking to maintain the singular term–general term distinction. However the question is decided, talk of universals is so widespread in logic and philosophy that the universal–particular distinction should not be ignored.

2. *Modal Logic*

In philosophy of religion, as elsewhere, one often hears it said of some claim not merely that it is true but that it is *necessarily* true. Thus, for example, it is sometimes claimed that it is necessary that God exists. But too often such claims are obscure, and if we are to evaluate them successfully, we need a clear characterization of what such expressions as 'necessary' and 'possible' mean. Often we do not literally say what we mean, as (1) and (2) below illustrate:

(1) It is necessary that you renew your driver's license before it expires.

(2) Food, shelter, and clothing are necessary.

(3) It is necessary that either today is Monday or today is not Monday.

Consider (1) and (2). Of course, it is not literally necessary that one renew a driver's license before it expires. Consider:

(1′) It is necessary that you renew your driver's license before it expires if you are to drive legally.

(1′) makes explicit an understood condition, which was probably left out of (1) because it is assumed that one will desire to drive and to drive legally. Consider:

(2′) It is necessary that if humans are to live comfortably they have food, shelter, and clothing.

(2′) makes explicit an understood condition left out of (2) (once again, probably because it is assumed that humans wish to live comfortably). (1′) and (2′) are examples of what is sometimes called conditional necessity. But it is perhaps more important to note that (1′), (2′), and (3) illustrate three somewhat different senses of 'It is necessary that'. (1′) and (2′) have the form:

$$\text{It is necessary that } (\Phi \rightarrow \Psi).$$

But the contained conditional is not the only reason that can be given for saying that they express conditional necessity. (1′) holds only on the assumption of certain legal conventions. It is possible for there to be states where licensing of drivers is optional. We may make this further condition explicit in:

(1″) It is necessary that if the state in which you drive requires by law that each driver be licensed, then if you are to drive legally you will renew your driver's license before it expires.

(2′) holds only on the assumption of certain causal conditions for comfortable living for humans. Certainly it is imaginable that there be a world in which humans need neither shelter nor clothing for comfortable living.

But (3) is not based on any assumption of conventions of causal conditions. There is no possible world in which (3) is false, for (3) is a statement of *logical* necessity. Philosophers, in so far as they are concerned with notions of possibility and necessity, are interested primarily in *logical* necessity and possibility. We shall therefore try to present a more careful characterization of these notions, bearing in mind that it is only the logical sense of possibility and necessity that this characterization is aimed at reflecting.

Let us begin by introducing '□' as a representation for 'It is necessary that' and '◇' for 'It is possible that'. We shall utilize the conventions for exhibiting the logical form of complex sentences adopted in Chapter I. '□' and '◇' are *modal operators;* we can point out several interesting relations which hold between sentences that are formed using these operators:

Sentences of the form:	are logically equivalent to sentences of the form:
1. ◇Φ	1. ~□~Φ
2. ◇~Φ	2. ~□Φ
3. □~Φ	3. ~◇Φ
4. □Φ	4. ~◇~Φ

Intuitively, what line 1 says is: To say it is possible that Φ is to say it is not necessarily the case that ~ Φ. Line 2 says: To say it is possible that ~ Φ is to say it is not necessarily the case that Φ. Line 3 says: To say necessarily ~ Φ is to say it is not possible that Φ. Finally, line 4 says: To say necessarily Φ is to say it is not possible that ~ Φ.

Several interesting entailment relations between sentences of different forms can now be noted:

Sentences of the form:	entail sentences of the form:
5. □Φ	5. Φ
6. (□(Φ → Ψ) & □Φ)	6. □Ψ
7. (□(Φ → Ψ) & ◊Φ)	7. ◊Ψ
8. □Φ	8. ◊Φ
9. Φ	9. ◊Φ

Line 5 says: If necessarily Φ, then Φ. Line 6 says: If necessarily Φ and, necessarily, Φ only if Ψ, then necessarily Ψ. Line 7 says: If possibly Φ and, necessarily, Φ only if Ψ, then possibly Ψ. Line 8 says: If necessarily Φ, then possibly Φ. Finally, line 9 says: If Φ, then possibly Φ.

We may also use our modal operators to express the fact, e.g., that it is *contingent* that Babe Ruth has hit more home runs in major-league play than any other player. For this is simply to say that it is neither logically necessary that he has nor logically necessary that he has not. The relationships among modalities of necessity, possibility, contingency, and impossibility are summarized in Figure 1 for any sentence abbreviated by 'P'.

Figure 2 represents relationships holding among modalities and truth values. Sentences of four different kinds are represented by the vertical lines 1, 2, 3, and 4. Modalities

If it is ___ that P	We write	or equivalently	and also it is ___ that P	but it is false that it is ___ that P	and it is ___ that ~P
necessary	□P	~◇~P	possible	contingent impossible	impossible
possible	◇P	~□~P	—	impossible	—
contingent	(~□P & ~□~P)	(◇~P & ◇P)	possible	necessary impossible	contingent possible
impossible	□~P	~◇P	—	necessary possible contingent	necessary

Figure 1

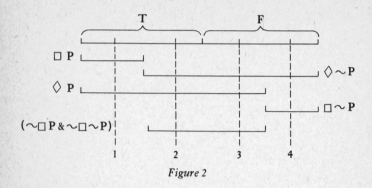

Figure 2

and truth values are represented by the horizontal lines, as indicated. For example:

$$P_1: \text{ All men are men}$$

is represented by the line at 1. That is, it is true that P_1, it is necessary that P_1, and it is possible that P_1. But it is not possible that not P_1, it is not necessary that not P_1, and it is not contingent that not P_1. Similarly, the following sentences are represented respectively by the lines at 2, 3, and 4.

P_2: The population of Boston exceeds 50,000.
P_3: The population of North Platte exceeds 1,000,000.
P_4: The second man to arrive was the first man to arrive.

We shall now attempt to strengthen the reader's intuitions concerning the meaning of 'It is necessary that'. Most of us readily agree that the world might have been different than it has been, that it could be different than it now is, and that it could be different than it in fact will be. We can think of alternatives to the actual world as possible, though not actual, worlds. Obviously the actual world is also a possible world. It is often helpful to think of 'It is necessary that' as meaning 'It is true in all possible worlds that '. Admittedly, this suggestion will not carry us very far unless some helpful explication of the concept of a possible world can be given. But for some purposes this concept can be helpfully explicated.

We can point out two classes of sentences such that each member of these classes is true in all possible worlds. (1) Sentences that are true in virtue of their form alone (i.e., all logical truths) are true in all possible worlds since the descriptive content of these sentences has no effect on their truth. (2) All sentences that are true in virtue *only* of what they mean without need to consider what the actual state of the world is are true in all possible worlds. (We assume here that the meanings of expressions in the language we are considering remain constant, regardless of what possible world is being considered.) Clearly the first set of sentences is included in this set, but this set contains sentences that are not true in virtue of their form alone. For example, 'All male siblings are brothers' and 'All red things are colored' are members of the second but not of the first class. Sentences of this second class are said to be analytically true. (Cf. VI, 2.)

These remarks based on the notion of possible worlds are only intended to aid the reader in understanding a very strong sense of 'It is necessary that' which is of considerable interest to philosophers. We have already seen that this phrase may be used when someone wishes to express a much weaker concept. Perhaps the most important point to be learned from this section is that one must be cautious in using modal language and that arguments and assertions which utilize modal language are often more difficult to understand than they initially seem to be.

Exercises

1. Which of the following sentences could be true? Explain your answers.
   - (a) 'Not all men are mortal' implies 'Some man is not mortal'.
   - (b) God created the world infers the world was created.
   - (c) 'The world was created' incorrectly implies 'God created the world'.
   - (d) John ought to return the book implies John can return the book.
   - (e) The fact that John believes that he exists infers the fact that John exists.

2. What does it mean to call a set of sentences consistent?

3. Suppose it is true that:

$$((P \rightarrow Q) \,\&\, (R \leftrightarrow P)).$$

Which of the following is true?
   - (a) Its being true that P is a necessary condition for its being true that Q.
   - (b) Its being true that P is a necessary condition for its being true that R.
   - (c) Its being true that P is a sufficient condition for its being true that R.
   - (d) Its being true that P is a sufficient condition for its being true that Q.

(e) Its being true that R is a sufficient condition for
its being true that Q.

4. Indicate for each use below of the verb 'to be' whether
the use is to assert identity, predication, class inclusion or
existence. Indicate possible ambiguities.
  (a) Whatever *is, is* right.
  (b) Black *is* the color of my true love's hair.
  (c) Husbands *are* men.

5. Discuss the following argument:
  (i) Pure-blooded Choctaw Indians are scarce.
  (ii) My great-uncle Joe is a pure-blooded Choctaw
  Indian.
  (iii) Therefore, my great-uncle Joe is scarce.

6. Let the domain of discourse be {1,2,3,4}.

Let A = {1,2}
  B = {3,4}
  C = {2,3,4}.

Which pairs of sets are mutually exclusive? Which groups
of sets are jointly exhaustive?

7. Discuss the following sentence with reference to the
traditional distinction between universals and particulars:

The Mona Lisa is beautiful; and surely if anything is beautiful, beauty is.

8. Using Figure 2, page 58, indicate for each of the following sentences (A) which vertical line represents it and
(B) what its truth value and modalities are:

(a) Telephones are widely used.
(b) Seven is greater than four.
(c) Eisenhower was President for seventeen years.
(d) Urban air has been polluted by industrial wastes.
(e) Smoking cigarettes regularly is extremely un-
healthy.
(f) Most women drive sports cars.
(g) George carved a spherical cube of wood.
(h) Edward's brother is his nephew's wife.
(i) Urban air is found in cities.

9. Give two examples each of sentences that are represented
by lines 1, 2, 3, and 4 of Figure 2, page 58.

IV

Assertions, Sentences, and Propositions

Philosophers typically are concerned in a number of ways with questions of truth. Thus, for example, in Chapter I we discussed the relationship between the truth of some sentences (the premises) and that of some other sentence (the conclusion) in an argument. Another philosophical inquiry about truth has to do with the meaning of the word 'true'. Thus one may ask what it means to say of some assertion that it is true. (Cf. IX, 8.) Still another question one may ask is "What is true?" But that question can be taken in at least two ways: (1) as an inquiry into what the facts about the world are—that is, an inquiry into which of the claims of physics, sociology, economics, and so forth, are true; or (2) as an inquiry into what *sorts* of things are true—that is, an inquiry into whether it is sentences, actions, assertions, or people that can have the property of being true. It is with the second question that we shall be concerned in this section. That question is one that must be answered, for if we do not know what kinds of entity can have truth value, we may not be able to tell whether or not some questions make sense when they are of the form 'Is x true?'—e.g., 'Is Smith's action true?'

The word 'true' appears in many contexts that are not of special concern to a philosopher interested in problems of truth. Consider a few examples:

(1) John is true blue.
(2) That material is true alligator, not a plastic imitation.
(3) My husband has always been true to me.

There is very likely some connection between these uses of 'true' and the concept of truth that philosophers have been interested in. But these examples are not typically of philosophical interest. The following conversation, on the other hand, contains a use of the predicate 'is true' in a context that may be used as a starting point for a philosophical examination of the concept of truth:

> Apprentice electrician: There is no point in going back to the truck for a voltmeter. I can check it with my fingers; 110 volts isn't going to hurt me.
> Journeyman electrician: That's true; but if it is 220 volts, the twenty-foot drop to the ground may be a bit jarring.

As this conversation indicates, we often use 'true' as a sort of me-too expression, a short way to say what has just been said or to agree with what has just been asserted. Thus one might say that the kind of thing that can be true or false is *assertions*. But if this answer is to provide insight into the concept of truth, we must ask what assertions are. Are they sentences, or are they actions? It is sufficient for our purposes to note that sentences and actions are indeed different sorts of things and that therefore the claim that assertions are the things that are true or false is subject to differing interpretations.

Asserting is something that people *do;* so we may say that assertions are a kind of action. But it is at least counter-intuitive to say that actions are the sorts of things that are true or false. We would not want to say that every action—e.g., John's robbing a bank—was either true or false. We would want a way to distinguish those actions that can be true or false from those that cannot. Thus it becomes clear that the claim that assertions are the things that are true or false is not unproblematical.

We have said that 'true' is often used to assert the same *thing* as has been said, to agree with *what has been asserted*. Perhaps we should have said that it is the product of an act of asserting—what is *asserted*—that is either true or false. Let us for the moment say that sentences are what is asserted and thus that it is sentences that are either true or false. This seems to give a clear answer to the second question about truth, since it seems to be clear what sentences are. But consider this: How many sentences are there in the box below?

A
> Peter is thirteen years old.
> Peter is thirteen years old.

Is there one sentence there or two? Philosophers concerned with language have settled this question by making a distinction between sentence *types* and sentence *tokens*. There are two sentence tokens in the box, but only one type. A written token is a collection of physical objects, in this case bits of paper marked with ink and arranged in a specified order with appropriate spacing. A written sentence token is made up of word tokens (which in turn are made up of letter tokens) and punctuation tokens. A spoken sentence token is probably best thought of as an event, a happening, of which people are usually made aware by vibrations in some physical medium. Consequently, one can observe that same written token many times, but a spoken token can never be reduplicated. Each token is a particular object or event. Written tokens can be copied, and spoken tokens can be reproduced by a tape recorder or copied by a skillful mimic; but two written tokens, no matter how much they look alike, are still two tokens. A spoken token and a re-production of it occur at different times and are two events, two tokens. But although the two tokens in the box are different tokens, they are obviously alike in many respects, so much so that we may often say that there is only one sentence in the box. The likeness of these tokens is often explained by saying that they instantiate, that is, are in-stances of, the same sentence type or that they are tokens of the same type. Sentence types are not physical objects that can be located in space and time; thus it was mislead-ing to say that there is one sentence type *in* the box. There is only one sentence type instantiated by the sentence tokens that are in the box. The same sentence type may also be instantiated in handwriting or in italic type, and it might be instantiated orally; thus two tokens can differ a great deal and still instantiate the same type. What is re-quired for two tokens to be of the same type is that they be composed of the same words in the same language in the same order. Nonetheless, just how much two tokens can differ while instantiating one type is not always clear.

If 'thirteen' in the first token had been misspelled, we would probably say that the tokens still instantiated the

same type. But a difference in one letter can be enough to
assure that two tokens instantiate different types; consider:

B   Charles is married to Jo*a*n.
    Charles is married to Jo*h*n.

But if it is sentences that are either true or false, is it
sentence types or sentence tokens? If it is sentence types
that can be true or false, we might say that the type instantiated by the token 'Peter is thirteen years old' is true
only at the time when Peter is actually thirteen years old.
But fixing the type a token instantiates does not fix the
reference of the terms in the token; that is, we do not know
who Peter is, we do not know to whom the name 'Peter'
refers. We have already said that tokens instantiating the
same type may differ from one another in many ways;
clearly they may be spoken or written at different times
and by different people. Different tokens instantiating this
same type may be used to refer to many different persons
named Peter, only some of whom will be thirteen years old.
Suppose tokens of this type appeared on the medical chart
of Peter Smith, who is thirteen years old, and on the chart
of Peter Brown, who is twenty years old. What then would
we say of the truth of the type? In one case Peter is thirteen
years old; in the other Peter is not. But we do not want to
say that the same sentence type is both true and false.

In discussing the possibility of types being true, we mentioned the idea of the reference of tokens; in fact, it was
tempting to say that the token that referred to Peter Smith
was true, while that which referred to Peter Brown was
false. Let us see whether sentence tokens provide a more

satisfactory answer to the question of what sorts of things
can be true or false.

We do not immediately face the same problem with
tokens that we faced with types, since it is unlikely that
'Peter' in any one token would refer to different Peters. A
particular token is written or uttered in a particular context, which aids in determining the reference of its terms;
for example, the token written on Peter Smith's medical
chart. But sometimes it is not possible to determine the
reference of a particular token. Is the first token in box A
above true or false? That token was used as an example,
and as such it has no context that aids us in establishing the
reference of 'Peter'; it was not written on someone's medical
chart, nor spoken at Peter Smith's birthday party. If we do
not know to whom 'Peter' refers, how can we decide
whether the token is true or false? Although we may be
convinced that 'Peter' does not refer to *more* than one person named Peter, have we any assurance that 'Peter' does
refer to *anyone* named Peter? The person responsible for
that token's being produced may not have had any person
named Peter in mind. If 'Peter' in this token does not refer
to anyone, what does it mean to say that the token is true?
We may well maintain that, even if tokens are generally
the things that are true or false, some tokens are neither
true nor false. This should not be particularly surprising,
since we began this discussion by talking about things that
are asserted in an act of assertion; and the first token in the
box above was not asserted, it was merely used in illustration. It may still be the case that all asserted tokens are
either true or false.

However, we should note that even if all asserted tokens
are either true or false, there is a serious difficulty in the
supposition that whatever is true or false is a sentence

token. For there will be sentence types that are not instantiated by any sentence token. (We cannot give an example
of one, for to do so would require instantiating it). If only
sentence tokens are true or false, then none of these unin-
stantiated types could be either true or false. Yet it seems
reasonable to speak, e.g., of mathematical truths that have
not ever been explicitly expressed.

At this point, it is well to reflect on the course of this
discussion. Because it seemed counter-intuitive to say that
actions can be true or false, we were led to say that it is
what is asserted—sentences—that can be true or false. And
because the question of the truth of a sentence type was
complicated by the fact that tokens of the same type can
have different references, we turned to sentence tokens. But
in addition to the difficulty that there seem to be more
things true or false than there are sentence tokens, we must
ask if it is any more plausible to say that these collections
of physical objects or events are true or false. Isn't it rather
what these things *mean* that is important in discussions of
truth? Suppose someone asserts that Φ entails Ψ and also
asserts Φ, expecting us to infer Ψ. Isn't it going to be important that Φ in 'Φ entails Ψ' means the same thing as Φ in
isolation? Surely something must be the same in the two
cases in order that the entailment may hold. But *what* must
be the same? The tokens obviously will be different, and
tokens of the same type can have different truth values. We
want not only tokens of the same type but tokens that mean
the same thing, have the same reference, and therefore have
the same truth value. Because of the importance of meanings in such considerations, philosophers have sometimes
said that logical relations, such as entailment, hold among
propositions, i.e., among the meanings of sentence tokens,
rather than among the tokens themselves and that these

meanings or propositions are the things that are true or false.[1]

If two English sentence tokens mean exactly the same thing, then it is said that they are synonymous and express the same proposition. For example, we may say that 'Not every dog is white' and 'It is not the case that every dog is white' express the same proposition. Whereas a single sentence type can be instantiated by tokens that have different meanings, a single proposition can be expressed by different tokens only when those tokens have the same meaning, since the meaning is the proposition expressed. Further, one proposition may be expressed by sentence tokens in different languages. Traditionally, one reason for introducing the notion of a proposition has been to explain the possibility of translation; it is presupposed that translation is possible only if two sentences in different languages have the same meaning. If an English sentence token can be translated into German without change in meaning, then the English token and the different token that is its German translation express the same proposition. Each token, being spoken or written in a particular language, is bound to that language; but propositions are not bound to any *particular* language.

Propositions are sometimes said to be timeless. That is to say, if propositions are what is true or false and if some particular proposition is true now, then it always has been and always will be true. Note that while any one written token may instantiate only one sentence type, it may ex-

---

[1] We do not directly discuss the claim that it is statements which are either true or false, since the word 'statement' has been ambiguously used in philosophical discussion. Statements have been taken to be acts of assertion, sentence tokens, sentence types, and propositions; but all of these notions have been discussed in this section. The same remarks apply to the word 'claim'.

press more than one proposition at different times. Imagine that we construct a letter by cutting sentence tokens out of magazines and pasting them onto a sheet of paper. It is quite possible for one of these tokens to express a different proposition in the magazine from the one that it expresses in the letter—i.e., to have a different meaning in each case. But the only way we have of saying what proposition a sentence token expresses is to produce another token, in the same or a different language, that is synonymous with the first token—i.e., to point to another token that has the same meaning and thus expresses the same proposition. If propositions are what is true or false, then this one token may be said to express a true proposition in the magazine and a false one in the letter. On the other hand, if tokens are what is true or false, we shall have one token that is both true and false, but at different times. We may say that the truth value of the token has changed, but this change has been made possible only by the fact that the token expresses first one proposition, then another. The truth values of the propositions expressed, however, have not changed.

Yet, there are difficulties inherent in asserting that it is propositions that are either true or false, because the concept of a proposition is not entirely precise. We have said that a proposition is the meaning of a sentence and that the sentence *expresses* the proposition. But consider the sentence 'It is cold out today'. If we say, once in winter and once again in summer, 'It is cold out today', then presumably what we have said in the winter is true and what we have said in the summer is false. Yet the sentence seems to have the same *meaning* in both cases. If we suppose that (1) the meanings are the same, (2) the propositions expressed are the meanings, (3) the truth values apply to the

propositions, and (4) whatever is true is not false and whatever is false is not true, then we seem to be forced to say
that the proposition expressed by 'It is cold out today' is
true and also not true. But this is a contradiction. We can
try to avoid this problem in at least two ways. We could
deny that propositions are meanings after all. But then we
would have to regard meanings and propositions as distinct
entities, thereby raising problems concerning the relations
between the meaning of a sentence and the proposition it
expresses. The denial that propositions are meanings offers
no insight into the claim that it is propositions that are
either true or false. We could instead hold the view that
propositions are meanings but deny that the meanings are
the same in the two cases referred to above. We would then
hold that the meaning is adequately specified only when
we specify time and location in each case. But this attempt
is open to the objection that it is only because the sentence
has the same meaning, whether it is spoken in summer or
winter, that it is false in 100° summer heat but true in 20°
winter cold. That is, if the sentence had one meaning when
spoken in winter and a different meaning when uttered in
summer, it might express a true proposition on both occasions. On either of these proposed alternatives, we are still
faced with the task—in general a troublesome one—of
identifying the proposition expressed by a given sentence.

Even if, in the above example, we could specify what
proposition was expressed by expanding the sentence so
as to include time and location, such a simple procedure
would not always succeed. Consider the sentence 'Salem
is in Massachusetts'. If 'Salem' refers to Salem, Massachusetts, then the proposition expressed by the sentence is true.
But if 'Salem' refers to Salem, Oregon, then the proposition

is false. How can we expand the sentence to make clear what proposition is expressed? It is not appropriate here simply to fill in time and place coordinates, since in this case the truth value of the proposition does not depend on the time or place it is asserted. If we expand the sentence to 'Salem, Massachusetts, is in Massachusetts', then we have specified the reference of 'Salem' and the proposition expressed is clearly true. But it is contingent that Salem is in Massachusetts, although it is necessary that Salem, Massachusetts, is in Massachusetts. Given the reasonable hypothesis that if two sentences express the same proposition, then one is contingent if and only if the other is, the proposed expansion does not express the same proposition as the original sentence did and does not show which proposition was expressed by 'Salem is in Massachusetts'.

There are of course other ways in which we may specify the reference of 'Salem', in an attempt to determine what proposition is expressed by the original sentence, and yet preserve the contingency of the original sentence. Consider, for example, 'The Salem that was founded in 1626 is in Massachusetts'. If this sentence expresses the same proposition as the first, then the first expressed a true proposition and 'Salem' therein refers to Salem, Massachusetts. However, it seems to be a reasonable assertion that if two sentences express the same proposition, then neither conveys more information than the other nor contains any assertion that the other does not. But if this is so, we cannot hold that 'Salem is in Massachusetts' and 'The Salem that was founded in 1626 is in Massachusetts' express the same proposition. Even if true, the first conveys, for example, no information in regard to the founding date of any city. And the second, if we suppose the conditions of utterance to be normal, is used to assert in part that there is one, and only one, Salem that was founded in 1626; the first, under normal circumstances, cannot be thus used.

Of course, we have not shown that it is altogether impossible to expand a sentence so as to make explicit what proposition is expressed by the original sentence. Neither have we shown that there can be no other way to determine what proposition is expressed by a given sentence. What we have shown is that the specification of what proposition a sentence expresses is in general no simple matter. Yet, in order for the claim that it is propositions that are true or false to be enlightening, there must be some way of making such a specification.

In discussing the question of what sort of thing is true, we have found ourselves faced with the contradictory claim that something is both true and not true. This seems to be a difficulty analogous to that which we face when we recognize that a fence which is white can be painted black all over, that whatever is black all over is not white, and that nothing is white and not white. The obvious solution to this difficulty is to recognize that the same thing can be white at one time and not white at another time. Why have philosophers been so reluctant to apply this simple solution to our present problem? The answer to this question may be of considerable interest to an historian of philosophy or to an historian of thought. It is sufficient for us to notice that we have no objection to saying that the fence has been changed when it is painted; but we saw that one sense that can be given to the claim that propositions are timeless is that propositions do not change in truth value.

A possible solution to our problem seems to be to take sentence types as true or false but add that they are not *simply* true or *simply* false; rather they are true at some specifiable time and in some specifiable language. It is not contradictory to assert both that sentence type S is true at time t_1 in language L_1 and that sentence type S is false at t_2 in language L_1 or false at time t_1 in language L_2. Of course, we cannot rest content with this solution unless all ambiguities of reference are eliminated. (Consider the discussion on page 67 with respect to 'Peter is thirteen years old'.) Such elimination, in natural languages as opposed to formal languages, is no simple task. It should be emphasized that this sort of relativization of the concepts of truth and falsity to time and language lends no credence whatsoever to the mistaken doctrine that something may be true for one person and false for another.

The question of just what sorts of things are true and false has not been settled here. We shall follow the practice of speaking simply of sentences as true or false. But it must be remembered that although this manner of speaking is here adopted for the sake of simplicity, the question of the vehicles of truth is a complex one indeed.

Exercises

1. Give examples of two tokens of the same type.

2. Give one reason against taking sentence types as true or false.

3. What is the relation between propositions and sentence tokens?

4. Illustrate two tokens of different types that express the same proposition.

V

Extensional and Intensional Sentences

Aristotle said long ago that it is important to distinguish between voluntary actions and those that are not voluntary, because praise and blame are bestowed on those that are voluntary but not on those that are not voluntary. This distinction is not always easy to make; in fact, our first attempts may seem to end in contradictions. Consider a simple example: Joan comes home two days early from a visit to her hometown. The same night her husband, Conrad, comes home very late and finds that he has forgotten his key and is locked out. He knows that he can get in through the bedroom window and does so. Joan awakens to see a man starting to climb through the window. She reaches into the drawer by the bed, pulls out a gun, shoots and wounds Conrad. Did Joan shoot Conrad voluntarily? She says that she did not; she didn't know that it was Conrad, and there is no reason to suppose that she is lying. On the other hand she admits that she voluntarily shot the man crawling in the window. But surely Joan's shooting Conrad and Joan's shooting the man climbing through the window were the same action. Thus, by a simple inference, we can conclude that

Joan shot Conrad voluntarily. Yet this directly contradicts
Joan's honest claim, which she can support with good reasons. A possible way out of this difficulty lies in making a
distinction between *intensional* and *extensional* sentences.

We begin by introducing several closely related terms
that are commonly used in discussions of synonymy and
related topics in philosophy of language. We may speak of
the *sense* and the *reference* of a word or phrase. We may
also speak of its *intension* and *extension* or, less commonly,
of its *connotation* and *denotation*. It is important to note
here that: (1) 'intension' and 'extension' as introduced here
are not to be confused with 'intensional' and 'extensional'
as introduced above; (2) 'intension', with an 's', is a technical term, not to be confused with the ordinary English
word 'intention', with a 't'; (3) 'connotation' and 'denotation' are not used in philosophical contexts as they often
are in English grammar books. With these cautions in mind,
we may proceed.

In philosophical usage, 'sense', 'connotation', and 'intension' are roughly equivalent, as are 'reference', 'denotation',
and 'extension'. To see what the distinction is between sense
and reference, consider the following example: The morning star and the evening star are the same planet. Thus the
phrases 'the morning star' and 'the evening star' both refer
to the same object, i.e., they have the same reference, denotation, and extension. But 'the morning star' and 'the evening
star' do not have the same meaning or sense, as can be
seen from the following argument. If one wishes to know
whether the morning star is identical with the morning star,
he would need only to reflect on the logical structure of the
sentence 'The morning star is identical with the morning
star'. His evidence, if any, would be from logic rather than
from astronomy (cf. VI). But consider the sentence 'The

morning star is identical with the evening star'. The evidence for this sentence comes from astronomical investigation. No one could have discovered that these two phrases referred to the same planet simply by reflecting on the meanings of the phrases.

This difference in relevant evidence indicates that the two sentences differ in meaning. Yet they differ only in that the second has the phrase 'the evening star' substituted for one occurrence of the phrase 'the morning star' in the first. The obvious reason why the sentences differ in meaning is that the phrases differ in meaning even though both refer to the same object. We might also have argued that these phrases differed in meaning while having the same reference, by noting facts like the following. A person may believe that Venus is the morning star without believing that Venus is the evening star and yet be said to understand the meaning of both these phrases. Similarly, someone may hope to see the evening star in his telescope without hoping to see the morning star. Thus two words or phrases can differ in meaning while referring to the same object, and the meaning of a word or phrase is seen to be something different from the object to which the word or phrase refers. As mentioned above, we call the meaning of a word or phrase its *sense* or *intension* and the object (or objects) to which the word or phrase refers its *reference* or *extension*. Words or phrases that mean the same thing, i.e., are synonymous, are called *intensionally equivalent;* words or phrases that have the same extension or reference are called *extensionally equivalent*. Our discussion of 'the morning star' and 'the evening star' has shown that phrases may be extensionally equivalent while differing in intension or meaning; if two terms are intensionally equivalent, however, then they must be extensionally equivalent.

So far, we have been speaking about words or phrases having intensions and extensions. But sentences, too, have meaning, and we may widen these notions to apply to sentences as well. We shall say that the intension of a sentence is its meaning—or in other words, the proposition it expresses. But what is the extension of a sentence? It is not clear that sentences refer to anything at all. Nonetheless, we say that the extension of a sentence is its truth value.[1] Thus sentences that express the same proposition are intensionally equivalent or synonymous, while sentences are extensionally equivalent if they have the same truth value. Note that the use of 'extension' in the case of sentences is somewhat different from its use for words or phrases. A connection between these two uses of 'extension' may be arrived at by reflecting that the extension (truth value) of a sentence depends in part on the extensions (references) of the phrases in the sentence.

We now summarize the above material graphically (p. 81). Note that if we consider meaningful sentences, (a) some sentences are called extensional (though all have extensions, i.e., all have a truth value), and (b) some sentences are called intensional (though all have intensions, i.e., all express propositions).

We may now proceed to the task of clarifying the distinction between intensional and extensional sentences.

In the discussion above, we touched on the relation between the extension or reference of a sentence (its truth or falsity) and the extension or reference of the terms that are used to make up that sentence. For example, in order to determine whether it is true that Peter is thirteen years

---

[1] This view, presented here for the sake of completeness, is derived from the writings of Gottlob Frege. See *Philosophical Writings of Gottlob Frege,* P. T. Geach and Max Black, translators (Oxford: Basil Blackwell, 1960) for Frege's development of these notions.

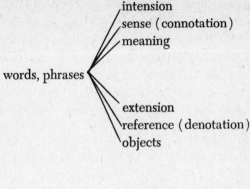

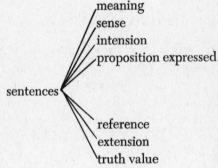

old, one would have to determine at least (1) to which Peter the name refers and (2) whether that Peter is included in the extension of the predicate 'is thirteen years old'—that is, whether the predicate is true of Peter. Suppose that the person to whom the name 'Peter' refers is the same person as the oldest son of John. Then if we substitute the description 'the oldest son of John' for the name 'Peter' in the sentence 'Peter is thirteen years old', the terms in the resulting sentence 'The oldest son of John is thirteen years old' have the same reference as the terms in the original sentence. Furthermore, the two sentences have the same extension, that is, the same truth value. Sentences like these, in which one can interchange extensionally equivalent terms one for another without producing a sentence of a different truth value from the first, may be called *extensional* sentences. To consider some sentences that are not extensional in this sense, let us suppose that Peter has a limited knowledge of astronomy and that, while the following sentence is true:

(1) Peter believes that Venus is the morning star,

this sentence is false:

(2) Peter believes that Venus is the evening star.

Sentence (2) was obtained from sentence (1), by replacing one description of Venus in (1) with another description that refers to the same heavenly body. If these two sentences were extensional, in the sense discussed above, they would not then differ in their truth value. Instead, sentences like (1) and (2) may be called *intensional.*

Let us generalize on this discussion by offering a rule of thumb to aid in distinguishing intensional from extensional sentences by pointing out one respect in which intensional sentences are like one another and at the same time different from extensional sentences:

A. Let Φ be any sentence, and let Ψ be any sentence that is obtained from Φ by replacing any name or description in Φ with any other name or description that refers to the same object. If for every such sentence Ψ, Φ and Ψ always have the same truth value, then they are extensional. But if there is any such sentence Ψ whose truth value differs from that of Φ, then Φ and Ψ are intensional.

Note that it may be possible to make extensionally equivalent replacements that do not change the truth value of
an intensional sentence. For example, suppose that the
following sentences are true:

(3) Peter believes that Venus is the only planet whose
diameter is 7600 miles.

(4) The oldest son of John believes that Venus is the
morning star.

The fact that (3) and (4) have the same truth value as
(1) does not show that these sentences are extensional.
Rather we see that they are intensional because there is
one sentence—sentence (2)—that can be obtained from
sentence (1) or (3) or (4) by interchanging terms that
refer to the same object, yet the truth value of sentence (2)
differs from that of (1), (3), and (4).

The failure of extensionally equivalent interchanges to
preserve truth value is one mark of an intensional sentence.
Let us consider another mark—the possibility that a name
or description in a sentence may not refer to something in
the world, even though the sentence is true:

(5) Peter is looking for the planet that is 1000 miles in
diameter.

(6) John hopes to ride Pegasus.

(7) Peter needs a good text on astronomy.

Contrast these sentences with the following:

(5a) Peter has found the planet that is 1000 miles in
diameter.

(5b) There is no planet that is 1000 miles in diameter.

(6a) John is not riding Pegasus.

(7a) Peter is reading a good text on astronomy.

Just as men could search throughout the middle ages for
the Holy Grail even though there was probably no such
object, so sentence (5) can be true even though (5b) is
true. But sentence (5a) entails that there is a planet which
is 1000 miles in diameter; that is, it entails something that
contradicts (5b). So (5a) and (5b) cannot both be true.
Similarly, John can hope to ride Pegasus whether there is
a Pegasus or not, whether the name 'Pegasus' refers to
anything that exists or not. And we could not tell from the
fact that Peter *needs* a good text on astronomy whether
there is such a text or not. But if it is true that Peter *is*
reading a good astronomy text, then such a text must exist.
Let us generalize on this mark of an intensional sentence
in another rule of thumb, which provides a sufficient but
not necessary condition for intensionality:

> B. Given a sentence Φ (not a statement of identity),
> containing names or descriptions $d_1, d_2, \ldots, d_n$, if
> it is not the case that either Φ or its negation $\sim \Phi$
> entails for *each* name or description d_i in Φ either
> that d_i does or that d_i does not refer to some object,
> then Φ is intensional.

Thus, (5a) is not shown by B to be intensional, because it
entails that something exists to which the name 'Peter' refers
and that, further, something exists that is referred to by
the description 'the planet which is 1000 miles in diameter'.
And (5b) is not shown to be intensional because it entails
that the same description fails to refer. But (5) *is* intensional, because neither it nor its negation entails either that
the description refers or that it fails to refer. (6a) does not
entail that 'Pegasus' does or does not refer, but since its
negation does entail that both John and Pegasus exist, it is
consistent with B that (6a) is extensional.

Rules A and B provide alternative rules of thumb in testing for intensionality, and there should thus be no conflict in result. Either rule, for example, will show that the following sentence is intensional:

(8) Peter hopes to be the first man on Venus.

Peter may hope that he will be the first man on Venus without hoping that he will be the first man on the evening star. And Peter could hope that he will be the first man on Venus even if there were no such planet as Venus. Thus, by both A and B, (8) is intensional. But if:

(8a) Peter is the first man to reach Venus.

then there must be something that he reaches. And if he is the first to reach Venus, then he is the first man to reach the evening star, the morning star, the only planet in our solar system whose diameter is 7600 miles, etc.—whether or not he knows or believes that these descriptions all denote Venus. Thus, (8a) is not shown to be intensional by B and is shown to be extensional by A.

Sentences about a person's beliefs, such as (1) and (2), are paradigms of intensional sentences; in fact, sentences about psychological phenomena generally provide the typical examples of intensional sentences.

In Chapter II, it was pointed out that the logical structure of such sentences as 'All bachelors are bachelors' cannot be adequately dealt with by propositional logic alone. Propositional logic is also inadequate to deal with the internal structure of intensional sentences, e.g.:

(9) John believes that painting is a pleasant recreation.

However, the following consideration may lead us to try treating intensional sentences by methods similar to those of propositional calculus. Consider:

(10) John believes that painting is *not* a pleasant rec-
     reation.

Since, typically, if (9) is true (10) will be false (and vice
versa), we may be tempted to treat such expressions as
'John believes that . . .' and 'Peter hopes that . . .' as
one-place sentential connectives similar to 'It is not the case
that . . .' But these connectives, which we may call intensional, will differ from negation because they are not truth-
functional sentential connectives; that is, we cannot construct for them a truth table that will enable us to compute
the truth value of 'John believes that P' on the basis of the
truth value of the sentence for which 'P' is an abbreviation.
That no such table is possible can be seen from consideration of sentences (1) and (2). 'Venus is the morning star'
and 'Venus is the evening star' are both true, but sentences
(1) and (2) differ in truth value even though each is the
result of applying the same one-place connective to sentences with the same truth value. Since we are no better
equipped to understand the structure of sentences using
non-truth-functional connectives than that of intensional sentences, little is to be gained by treating expressions like
'John believes that . . .' as connectives.

Further, it should be noted that the methods of analysis
provided by the predicate calculus do not seem to be adequate to reveal the features of the internal structure of
intensional sentences such as we have been discussing.

If a sentence is extensional, then inferences of the following form are valid, according to the rules of inference of
predicate calculus:

> The dog bites Jim.
> Jim is Joan's only son.
> Therefore, the dog bites Joan's only son.

But an inference of precisely the same form is invalid if one of the premises is an intensional sentence. Consider:

> Peter believes that x = y.
> y = z.
> Therefore, Peter believes that x = z.

Both premises of this argument can be true and still the conclusion be false (as exemplified by (1) and (2) above and, similarly, by the argument with which we introduced this section). We cannot infer from 'Joan's shooting the man crawling in the window was voluntary' and 'The man crawling in the window was Conrad' that 'Joan's shooting Conrad was voluntary'.

Although we now have some tests for intensionality, it would be a mistake to assume that we can always tell easily whether or not a given sentence is intensional. Consider, for example:

> (11) John loves Mary.

It is open to question whether or not (11) entails that Mary exists. Moreover, if Mary is the bank teller, and John knows the bank teller but doesn't realize that she and Mary are one, it is open to question whether or not replacement of 'the bank teller' for 'Mary' in (11) will preserve the truth value of (11). Thus, on both tests, it is unclear whether or not (11) is intensional.

We have noted that intensionality is a mark of sentences about psychological phenomena. One might therefore suggest that (11) is intensional because it concerns love, surely a psychological phenomenon. But this would beg the question of whether or not sentences about psychological phenomena are all really intensional. To answer that question, the intensionality of sentences must be determined inde-

pendently of whether or not they concern psychological phenomena.

In any case, not all sentences that are intensional by
virtue of tests A and B are obviously sentences about psychological phenomena. Thus:

> (12) It is possible that Venus is not the morning star.
> (13) It is necessary that Venus is Venus.

are both true. But if we interchange the two terms that
refer to Venus, we get:

> (12a) It is possible that Venus is not Venus.
> (13a) It is necessary that Venus is the morning star.

and both of these are false. Thus (12), (12a), (13), and
(13a) are intensional by rule A. Yet they do not seem to
involve psychological phenomena.

Exercises

1. Give an example of both an extensional sentence and an
   intensional sentence. Establish by interchange of expressions having the same extension that the second is intensional.

2. Does sameness of extension guarantee sameness of intension? Illustrate.

3. What is the extension of:
   - (a) 'Lyndon Johnson'
   - (b) 'The President of the United States of America
     in 1967'
   - (c) 'The King of France in 1967'.

VI

The Analytic-Synthetic and
A Priori–A Posteriori Distinctions

1. Introduction

The distinctions to be discussed below were first systematically set forth in the eighteenth century by Immanuel Kant, but they were implicit in the works of many of his predecessors.

It requires little reflection to convince oneself that the criteria we employ and the kinds of evidence we cite for the truth of particular claims vary markedly from case to case.

Suppose, for example, that we wish to discover whether the following claims are true:

    (a) All animals are animals.
    (b) The pear trees are in bloom.

In the latter case, one may well go to the place where the pear trees grow and look for blossoms, whereas the truth of the first sentence is evident merely upon an examination of its logical structure. The only evidence one might cite for (a) would be from a logic text, but the request for evidence seems out of place. The thing we do not do is go out in search of animals to see if they are animals.

To take a more interesting example, consider:

(c) God exists.

Traditionally, this claim has been supported or denied on widely divergent grounds. Some have insisted that (c) follows deductively from logically true premises, others that God's existence must be postulated to account for the world as we observe it to be, still others that because, in their view, (c) cannot be refuted or proved on the basis of the evidence of the senses, it is a meaningless claim.

These few examples are sufficient to suggest a host of philosophically interesting questions. What criteria of truth are relevant to the claims of theology or of physics? What kinds of evidence confirm the claims of natural science or ethics or the social sciences? And how is such evidence related to the corresponding claims? What sorts of things can be known by reason alone, without reference to sense experience? And so on.

The distinctions that follow were propounded not in order to answer such questions, but in an attempt to help clarify them and make them more precise.

2. *Analyticity*

(1) $(P \& (P \rightarrow Q)) \rightarrow Q$.
(2) Queen Elizabeth II is identical with Queen Elizabeth II.
(3) A brother is a male sibling.
(4) All brothers are males.
(5) Some bachelors are married.

The sentences above share this property: Their truth or falsity can be determined by an examination of their logical form and perhaps of the meanings of the words used to express them as well.

The first sentence is a tautology. The second has the logical form a = a and is thus logically true. By replacing 'male sibling' in (3) with its synonym 'brother', (3) can be reduced to a logical truth. Thus, the truth of (3) follows from the meanings of the words; that is, by interchanging synonyms for synonyms, we can convert (3) into a sentence, the form of which is obviously that of a truth of logic. The same is true of (4). Since brothers are male siblings, (4) is equivalent to 'All male siblings are males', which again has the form of a truth of logic. The meaning of the predicate in (4) is part of the meaning of the subject; (4) is a partial analysis of the term 'brother'. Finally, (5) is seen to be false once we consider the meaning of 'bachelor' and the logical form of the sentence.

Such sentences are said to be *analytic*.[1] Analytically true sentences are thus of two kinds—those [like (1) and (2)] which can be seen to be truths of logic, merely by inspection of their logical form, and those [like (3) and (4)] which can be seen to be logical truths by interchanging synonyms for synonyms and then examining the logical forms of the

[1] In Chapter II, some reasons were given for claiming that propositions rather than sentences are true or false. Thus, one may want to claim that it is propositions which are analytic or synthetic. This view is further motivated by the fact that criteria for analyticity depend heavily on word meanings and synonymy, so that sentences that have the same meanings (or express the same propositions) will be alike in analyticity. In this chapter, as throughout the book, we follow common usage in calling *sentences* analytic or synthetic. But, of course, the possibility remains open that it is the propositions expressed by these sentences that are analytic.

resultant sentences. Analytically false sentences are those
that are self-contradictory. As before, synonyms may have
to be replaced by synonyms to make evident the fact that
a sentence is self-contradictory.[2]

Another way to make the same distinction is to say that
the denial of an analytically true sentence is self-contradictory.

All sentences that are not analytic are called *synthetic*.
Some examples follow:

(6) Queen Elizabeth II was born in 1926.
(7) John has three brothers.
(8) It is often the case that bachelors own sports cars.
(9) The Earth is flat.

Neither synthetic sentences nor their denials are self-contradictory. Their truth or falsity cannot be determined by word
meanings and logical form alone. Crudely put, a synthetic
sentence has an extralogical content, and we must look
beyond the analysis of the meanings of the words involved
to settle its truth value. To assert that a particular synthetic
sentence is true is to assert that one of two mutually exclusive but logically possible states of affairs (described by
the sentence and its denial) is actually the case.

3. *The* A Priori

Setting aside temporarily the analytic–synthetic distinction, we can divide all sentences into two groups according
to whether or not they can be known to be true or false
without consulting experience. Sentences of the type that can
be refuted or confirmed only by experience (i.e., on the

---

[2] Often 'analytic' is used for 'analytically true', i.e., often 'S is analytic'
is intended to entail 'S is true'.

basis of observation) are called *a posteriori*. They are to be distinguished from sentences that can be known to be true (or false) without empirical evidence; these latter are *a priori* sentences. Thus, an *a priori* sentence is such that we can conceive of nothing that would count as evidence against it.

Examples of *a posteriori* sentences are easily found:

(10) It rained yesterday.
(11) It looks like rain.
(12) It will rain tomorrow.

All these are of the type of claim whose truth (or probability of being true) is to be found only by consulting our experiences.

But consider the mathematical equation:

$$(13)\ 5 + 7 = 12$$

What experience will refute or confirm (13)? If we put five apples into a basket, add seven more, and then count eleven apples in the basket, has (13) been refuted or cast into doubt? Clearly not. We shall seek some physical explanation or counting error and continue to consider (13) true. (13) is thus a paradigmatic example of an *a priori* sentence.[3]

---

[3] In ordinary discourse we often use '*a priori*' to mean 'independent of some particular experience' rather than 'totally independent of experience', as we are using it here. An example of this ordinary use is 'He should have known *a priori* that she would get angry with him for breaking the date'. That is, he should have known what her reaction would be prior to the actual *particular experience* of breaking the date.

Note too that to say that something can be known *a priori* is not to say that it can be known before any experience. Of course, we can have no knowledge of any kind before we have had experiences.

4. The A Priori Synthetic, Etc.

We are now in a position to construct a table illustrating the four combinations of the above criteria and the kinds of sentences that fall under them.

	A Priori	A Posteriori
Analytic	I. P or not P. All dogs are animals.	II.
Synthetic	III. Every event has a cause.	IV. The book is red.

Clearly, there are no *a posteriori* analytic sentences (group II) because analytic sentences are true by virtue of the meanings of their words alone, so that neither refutation nor confirmation by experience is possible. Therefore, all analytic sentences are *a priori* (group I).

Group IV comprises those sentences whose truth does not follow from word meanings and logical form but from experience. Examples of such 'empirical' claims are, of course, easy to find. Particular observational and predictive claims of natural science, as well as the bulk of our everyday conversation, belong to this group.

As may be expected, the most controversial category is group III, synthetic *a priori* sentences. Sentences of this type are not merely analyses of words, nor are they true on logical grounds alone; they say something about the world of our experience, and yet they are known independently of empirical evidence. Leaving aside the controversy for the moment, we may justify the example given, as follows:

(14) Every event has a cause.

The negation of (14) is not self-contradictory, therefore, (14) is not analytic. And yet its truth is independent of experience because we accept no experience as a refutation of it. That is, we may be unable to find the cause of a particular event; this does not lead us to postulate, however, that it was uncaused, but merely that we are ignorant of the cause. Some philosophers have held that if Φ is any *a priori* sentence abbreviated by 'P', then it is necessary that P. This claim is true if Φ is an analytic sentence. (Cf. III, 2, p. 53.) If it is to be necessarily true that P for some synthetic sentence, then that synthetic sentence must be true in all possible worlds. Whether it can be that a synthetic sentence is true in all possible worlds is a point of major philosophical dispute.

Though it is sometimes asserted that the analytic–synthetic and the *a priori–a posteriori* distinctions are in reality one distinction (and that only groups I and IV are legitimate), such a view requires careful arguments for its support. The distinction between analytic and *a priori* is at least nominally clear and should not be blurred. The criterion for analyticity has to do with logical structure and word meanings, while the criterion for something's being *a priori* is its relation to evidence and experience.

Of course, even when the distinctions are clear and precise, we may have trouble deciding the status of particular sentences. As a final example, consider the following:

(15) All swans are white.

Suppose this assertion is made by a biologist soon after the discovery and naming of the species 'swan' and before black swans have yet been observed. The status of (15) may be in doubt. If it is an *a posteriori* synthetic sentence, then it is only probably true and the appearance of one black swanlike bird will refute it. On the other hand, we may take (15) as *a priori* analytic, expressing one of the properties necessary for a bird's being a swan. Then the black swanlike bird may be denied the title 'swan' and categorized as a member of a different though related species. (Or we may amend the defining characteristics to include black as well as white swans—as in fact we do.)

5. *Some Contemporary Views*

In the 200 years since Kant wrote about these distinctions, they have never ceased to play a significant role in philosophical inquiry. As we shall indicate in section 6 below, some of the problems recurring in philosophy, particularly since Descartes, can be formulated directly in terms of the analytic–synthetic, *a priori–a posteriori* distinctions. In view of this, it is not surprising that much work has gone into the attempt to clarify these key concepts and to test the validity of the distinctions.

Some have asserted that there is, in principle, a fundamental imprecision in the concept of synonymy, which is fatal to the analytic–synthetic distinction. We have seen that there are two types of analytically true sentences: (a) those like 'Either today is Monday or it is not the case that today is Monday', whose truth is guaranteed by their logical form alone, and (b) those like 'Bachelors are unmarried', which can be shown to be logically true sentences by the interchange of synonyms for synonyms (in this case by the replacement of 'bachelor' with 'unmarried adult male'). Thus, to show that a sentence is analytic in this second way requires that we be able to decide with precision which words and phrases are synonymous; and we must be able to pick out these synonyms independently of any recourse to the idea of analyticity. For we cannot say, on pain of circularity, that two predicate expressions abbreviated by 'S' and 'F' are synonyms if and only if '(x) (Sx ↔ Fx)' is an *analytically true* sentence. But the problem of explaining just what synonymy is then arises. The most obvious attempt at solving this problem is the suggestion that synonymous words are those that can be substituted anywhere for one another without changing the truth value of the sentences into which the substitutions are made. For example, if (16) is true, then so is (17):

(16) Charlie is an unmarried adult male.
(17) Charlie is a bachelor.

But this test will not really work. If we consider certain intensional contexts (Cf. V), we cannot tell whether or not this test for synonymy has been passed unless we already know if we are dealing with synonyms. For example:

(18) Necessarily all bachelors are bachelors

is true. But our conviction that:

(19) Necessarily all bachelors are unmarried male adults

is true depends on our belief that 'bachelor' and 'unmarried male adult' are synonymous. If we did not think so, we would be reluctant to call (19) true. But a test for synonymy that requires us to know already what is synonymous is of no help. Recall that our initial effort was to be completely explicit and precise about what analyticity is.

That led us to consider what synonymy is, and our first attempt at answering the question failed. Other attempts have fared little better.

Those who have become impressed with the difficulty—or perhaps impossibility—of determining just which expressions are synonymous have naturally tended to be skeptical of the possibility of drawing a precise line between analytic and synthetic sentences. Of course, there are some sentences that are clearly synthetic and others whose analyticity no one would deny; but between these extremes may lie many sentences that appear to be analytic or synthetic but that cannot be placed with certainty into one category or the other. It is also asserted by some that the *a priori–a posteriori* distinction stands or falls with the analytic–synthetic distinction, while others hold that the former distinction may be maintained even though the latter should be given up.

Such controversies are not yet settled, and it is not the purpose of this section to explore them further. Rather, these contemporary views have been mentioned to emphasize the fact that the definitions of 'analytic', '*a priori*', etc., given in sections 2–4 above, are those traditionally given and are not to be taken as precise or adequate to all the work they are called upon to do. At best, what has been explained above can serve as a starting point for further inquiry; and these distinctions, though rough, can be used to shed some light on some of the perennial philosophical issues.

6. *Empiricism and Rationalism*

The distinctions we have been discussing help to make clear the fundamental difference between empiricism and rationalism. This difference can be set forth quite simply. Rationalists hold that there are synthetic sentences which are *a priori*, and they typically try to prove that certain basic assertions do have this status. Empiricists, on the other hand, insist that every true sentence is either analytic or else synthetic and *a posteriori*.

This dichotomy is especially clear in the case of Hume and Kant. It was largely in an attempt to provide an alternative to Hume's empiricism and the skepticism to which it led him that Kant developed the analytic–synthetic distinction and the concept of *a priori* knowledge. Since the eighteenth century, the formulation of the empiricist–rationalist controversy in terms of that distinction has remained virtually unaltered. (As mentioned in section 5 above, some doubt has recently been cast on the precision of the analytic–synthetic distinction; and this may lead to a reformulation of the point at issue.)

Further, the views of the rationalists and empiricists who preceded Hume and Kant can also be characterized according to their stand on the existence of *a priori* synthetic knowledge, although, generally, they did not explicitly employ the analytic–synthetic distinction.

The point here is not merely to label opposing sides of a long-standing philosophical controversy, but to indicate the essential difference between these two positions. At the same time, one must be careful not to overlook the significant differences between proponents of a single school. Descartes and Kant were both rationalists, according to the criterion we are using, but there are many important differences between their views.

Exercises

1. Give an example of an analytic sentence, an *a priori* false sentence, and an *a posteriori* true sentence.

2. What is the criterion of syntheticity?

3. What role does empirical investigation play in the determination of the truth or falsity of an analytic sentence?

4. Can there be analytic *a posteriori* sentences? Why or why not?

5. a. Suppose that 'gold' is defined as 'the yellow, malleable metal soluble in aqua regia'. Then what is the status of the claim that gold has an atomic weight of N? (That is, is the sentence analytic, synthetic–*a posteriori*, or what?)

   b. If we redefine 'gold' as 'that substance whose atomic weight is N', then what is the status of our original statement that gold is yellow, metallic, malleable, and soluble in aqua regia?

VII

Definition and Philosophical Analysis

1. Definition and Explication

A major technique of analytic philosophy is to try to formulate precisely the meanings of terms that, for one reason or another, are of special interest. This sort of philosophical activity dates back to the Greeks and their attempts to discover the nature of beauty, knowledge, justice, and goodness. Our present-day efforts to analyze such terms as 'good' and 'right' are the modern counterpart to the ancients' search for the essence of virtue and goodness. Thus, to say to a philosopher, "Define your terms. Tell me what you mean by 'good', and then we can begin to do ethics," is to misunderstand completely the nature of analytic philosophy. For the philosopher who can specify precisely what the meaning of 'good' is has already achieved some of the purposes with which one may set out to do ethics. Yet it is not as if we do not know at all what 'good' means. If that were so, then we would have no basis for objecting when someone told us, for example, that 'good' means the same as 'weighs between 7 and 34 pounds'. We know that this is not what 'good' means, because, as speakers of English, we have an intuitive understanding of the word. But that is not at all the same as being able to provide a precise and well-formulated definition of the term. Rather, we evaluate proposed definitions by comparing them with our intuitive understanding.

The dictionary, of course, provides definitions of all the terms that interest us. But dictionary definitions are not the kind that are of interest to philosophy, first, because dictionaries usually tell how words are used and, second, because dictionary definitions are circular. Let us now see how these two characteristics of dictionary definitions limit their usefulness in philosophy.

First, remember that we are seeking the meanings of terms. But telling how a word is used does not altogether give its meaning, because the use of a word is not the same as its meaning. Of course, in general, words could not be used the way they are if they didn't have the meanings they have, and they would not have the meanings they have if they were used differently. Use and meaning are thus closely related. But they are not quite the same. Consider the word 'angel'. We may *use* the word to describe an exceptional woman, but we don't intend to suggest that the woman literally *is* an angel. Rather, we are using the word metaphorically, in a way that depends on its literal meaning. We intend to suggest that the woman has certain angel-like qualities. It is just because the word 'angel' *means* what it does that we can use it in this way to describe something that is not really an angel.

The second limitation of dictionary definitions has to do with their circularity. Suppose, as an aesthetician, I am concerned to discover the nature of aesthetic value. I may begin by seeking the meaning of 'beautiful'. If I am told that 'x is beautiful' means 'x has beauty', I have been given a definition that surely everyone would agree is correct.

But it is of no philosophical value, because it defines the word 'beautiful' in terms of the notion of beauty, and that is just what we set out to analyze. The definition has led us right back where we started: It is circular.

Some definitions are circular in a less obvious way. For example, someone may suggest as a definition of 'x is beautiful' the expression 'x enjoys the characteristic of positive aesthetic merit'. The circularity here is not as apparent as in the previous case. But a moment's reflection reveals that the term we are interested in is defined in terms of a concept we do not understand, and, as if that alone were not enough to make the definition unsatisfactory, it was the attempt to understand that very concept that led us to seek the meaning of 'beautiful'. Thus here, too, we are led back to the place where we began; the circle is a bit larger, but it is nonetheless a circle. Even though they are ultimately circular, dictionary definitions are often helpful, because we usually understand the words used to define the term in question. But that dictionary definitions are always circular if followed far enough cannot be denied, because this circularity is guaranteed by the very attempt to define *each* word in the language in terms of other phrases in the language. Indeed, ultimate circularity can only be avoided by paying a price: The cost is that we must leave some words in the language undefined. Then the remaining words can be defined in terms of these *primitive* (i.e., undefined) expressions.

At this point, we should note that the word 'definition' is used ambiguously. That is, if we seek the meaning of A, and we are told that A means the same as B, we may speak of B as the definition of A. But we may also speak of the entire expression 'A means the same as B' as a definition. Since, in doing analytic philosophy, we wish to be as clear and precise as possible, we must find a way to eliminate the possibility of confusion arising from this ambiguity in the word 'definition'. We thus distinguish A and B as follows: We call the term that is defined the *definiendum*. In this case A is the definiendum. The term that gives the meaning of the definiendum—in this case, B—is called the *definiens*. We call the entire expression 'A means the same as B' a definition. Equivalently, we may say that A is equal to B *by definition*, which we abbreviate as: A $=_{df}$ B, writing the definiendum on the left and the definiens on the right.

It is a common opinion among people unfamiliar with analytic philosophy that the solution of philosophical problems is 'just a matter of definition'. They observe that any conclusion can be made to follow if one is permitted to define terms at will. For example, if I wish to show that causes must precede their effects in time, and I define 'cause' as 'an event that results in a later event', the conclusion I want is guaranteed by the definition. But the crucial point here is that one is *not* free to define terms at will. On the contrary, there are criteria that a definition must meet if it is to be philosophically acceptable. Thus, merely finding a definition that will support the desired conclusion is not enough. The definition must also meet the criteria, and the criteria make tasks that are 'just a matter of definition' very difficult indeed.

We have already seen what some of the criteria for definition are. First, definitions must be in accord with intuitive understanding of the definiendum. This criterion is difficult to meet, in practice, because it requires that the definiens must preserve the many meaning connections that the definiendum has with other words in the language. To illustrate: If we are trying to provide an adequate definition of 'motive', we must seek to insure that our definition does not entail that other closely connected words such as 'action' or 'desire' must be defined in ways that are contrary to our intuitive understanding of these latter terms. Or, to take a more detailed example, suppose we claim that the correct definition of 'evil' is (i) 'that which is contrary to God's law'. Although this definition may not obviously conflict with our intuitions about the meaning of 'evil', we must realize that it places certain constraints on what we can (consistently) mean by 'God', 'God's law', and 'contrary'. It may be that our intuitive understanding of the word 'God' (e.g., 'the omnipotent creator of the universe') is such that it is incompatible with definition (i)—because, for example, an omnipotent being does not ordain laws that can be broken. This line of reasoning raises questions about what we mean by 'omnipotent', and so on. In this way, the search for a philosophically adequate definition of a single expression almost always leads to a consideration of the meanings of many other related expressions.

In addition, philosophical definitions must not be circular, and the definiens must be expressed in language we can understand, or the definition is of no use. Besides, if we do not understand the definiens, there may be a hidden circularity in the definition. These criteria, in most philosophically interesting cases, are either very hard or impossible to meet. Consequently, the technique of *explication* has been developed as an alternative to definition.

The primary difference between explication and definition is that the criterion of accord with intuitive understanding is weakened in the former case. Outside of that, explication is much like definition. In fact, by analogy with definition, we introduce the technical terms *explicandum* and *explicatum* to refer respectively to the term we explicate and to the term or phrase we provide as a substitute for it. In seeking an explication for a term, we wish to capture as much of the meaning as we can characterize precisely. Thus, while we do insist on accord with intuitive understanding, we permit some deviation in the interest of gaining precision. For example, if we wish to explicate 'true', we might try as an explicatum the phrase 'in correspondence with the facts', even though this explicatum does not capture the meaning of 'true' as it is used in, say, 'a true Rembrandt' or 'a true woman'.

2. *Further Methods of Analysis*

Finding definitions or explications for philosophically important terms is not, of course, one of the primary goals of philosophy. It is, rather, a technique used in the pursuit of those goals. There are many other techniques that play a prominent part in philosophical analysis. Providing a *counterexample*, for instance, is a simple yet essential technique. A counterexample is merely an example which illustrates that a given general assertion is false. Consider the assertion that no United States President has ever been a Catholic. The fact that John F. Kennedy was both a Catholic and a United States President is a counterexample to that assertion. Or consider the assertion that no state is larger than Texas. The fact that Alaska is a state and is larger than Texas is the counterexample to that assertion. Similarly, if I assert that knowledge $=_{df}$ belief—that is, that 'belief' means the same as 'knowledge'—then the fact that one may be said to believe something, yet not to know it (if, for example, what he believes is false), provides a counterexample to my assertion that 'belief' means the same as 'knowledge'. We call such an illustration a counterexample to the definition.

Another important philosophical technique is that of *re-ductio ad absurdum*. That is, we show a position to be unacceptable by showing that it leads to—or can be reduced to—something absurd or clearly unacceptable for some other reason. For example, consider the assertion that there is no reason for keeping a promise. We apply the technique as follows. We consider what 'There is no reason to keep a promise' means by considering what a promise is. A promise, by its very nature, is obligatory. If someone makes a promise, then he has an obligation to keep it. Of course, something may happen to override that obligation; that is, there may be strong reasons not to keep the promise. But there is always some reason to keep it, simply because, as a prom-ise, it involves an obligation to do something, and being obliged to do something is a reason for doing it. The asser-tion we began with was that there is no reason for keeping a promise. But we have now seen that a promise is by its very nature something which there is a reason to keep. So the assertion comes down to saying that there is no reason to do something which by its very nature there is a reason to do. Since this is absurd, the claim must be rejected—*if* our argument is valid *and* our assumptions about the nature of promises are acceptable.

Finally, let us consider a somewhat more detailed illus-tration of philosophical analysis. The concept of causation is a prominent subject of philosophical inquiry. Consider the assertion that the same cause can have many effects. If we wish to be in a position to judge whether or not this assertion is true, we must first become clear about what it means. But its meaning is really not clear at all in spite of the fact that it may at first glance appear to be a simple assertion. In fact, we can distinguish a number of different ways in which it may be taken; and it may turn out that whether it is true or false that the same cause can have many effects depends on which way we take it. This situation is a standard one in analytic philosophy, where we are often faced with the task of evaluating an assertion that is actually ambiguous.

If we wish to understand the assertion in question, we must first achieve some clarity about the terms used. If we have no understanding of the word 'cause', then we cannot understand an assertion about causes. The first thing we note is that the word 'cause' is itself used ambiguously. That is, we sometimes speak of a *particular* event as a cause, as when we say 'When you went out without a hat, that (your going out last night without a hat) caused your cold'. But sometimes we speak of a *kind* of event as a cause, as when we say 'Going out without a hat causes colds'. Here we are not speaking of any particular event but of the entire class of events of a certain kind—the class of events that can be described as instances of going out without a hat. Now we can distinguish particular events (e.g., *your* going out without a hat *last* night) from kinds of events (e.g., going out without a hat). We can give a name to a particular event—let us refer to your going out last night without a hat as 'p'. Thus, we can say that p caused your cold. Let us also give a name to the kind of event in question. We shall say that an event is an event of kind A if it is an instance of going out without a hat. Thus, p is an event of kind A. There is just one p; it is a particular event. But there can be any number of events of kind A.

Now we are in a position to see the ambiguity in the claim 'The same cause can have many effects'. First, we see that the phrase 'the same cause' could refer to a *particular* event. An example might be p—your going out without a hat last night. One might then say that p can have many effects. But the phrase 'the same cause' may refer to causes of the same kind. Thus, if I too go out without a hat and I get a cough, one may say that the cause of my cough is the same as the cause of your cold. That is *not* to say that event p caused my cough. Rather, it is to say that my cough and your cold were both caused by events of the same kind, kind A.

We shall now distinguish two senses of the assertion in question. 'The same cause can have many effects' may mean:

(1) Two or more different events of the same type (e.g., A) can have effects of different types (e.g., coughs or colds).

(2) One event (e.g., p) can have many effects.

But (2) is itself ambiguous, because the phrase 'many effects' is in need of analysis. For example, if we say that p can have many effects, we may mean that the event p can result in a reprimand from your wife when you return, *and* a cold tomorrow, *and* loss of hair later. We are saying that one event (e.g., p) can have many subsequent effects (say, a, b, and c). On the other hand, we may mean that there are several different possible events any one of which could result from p, depending on the circumstances. For example, p could result in your getting a cold if it rains, *or* your winning a bet (e.g., that if you leave your hat at home it will not rain) if it doesn't. Thus, we are saying that one event (e.g., p) could result in one of many effects (b or d or e), depending on what happens. Thus (2) may mean:

(2a) One event (e.g., p) can have many subsequent effects, or

(2b) One event (e.g., p) could have various outcomes, depending on the circumstances.

We shall not carry the analysis any further, nor shall we be concerned with evaluating assertions (1), (2a), and (2b). Rather, we intend the analysis carried out so far to provide an illustration of actual philosophical activity and an example of the care with which such activity must be performed.

Exercises

1. Give an example of a plausible definition; identify the *definiendum* and *definiens*.

2. What are three criteria of adequacy for definition? Give examples of purported definitions each of which fails to meet one or more of the criteria you have cited.

3. Show by counterexample that some claim is false.

4. Explain the argumentative technique of *reductio ad absurdum*.

VIII

Reading and Writing Philosophy

1. *Reading Philosophy*

The fact that philosophical writing is typically discursive, and sometimes of great literary merit, must not mislead one into thinking that philosophy books can be digested rapidly or understood on first reading. Indeed, the student is well advised to approach a philosophy book much as he would approach a physics text or an essay in mathematics.

It is impossible, of course, to lay down a set of rules about how one must read philosophy. Every person should develop his own method of reading and understanding written material. Therefore, the following remarks should be regarded as a suggested approach to the reading of philosophy, setting forth what will generally be found to be the minimum requirements for understanding a piece of philosophical discourse.

A. Read the work through to the end, sympathetically, in order to become familiar with the organization of the book, the author's style, and the major problems to which the book is addressed.

B. Reread the book more carefully; try to isolate the issues and arguments.

C. Read the book in detail, proceeding slowly and analyzing each argument as it arises. One may want to outline certain passages or translate particular arguments into the notation of symbolic logic in order to clarify their structure.

D. Reread the book *in toto* to grasp the overall aims and conclusions of the author and to evaluate the consistency of his argument. It is only at this point, after each component argument has been mastered, that the work can be completely understood.

Philosophy, like most technical writing, must be read *actively*. One must carry on a silent dialogue with the author, questioning him at every turn and accepting his conclusions only after they have been carefully tested. The following are some questions that should be kept in mind while reading, particularly when one is analyzing the arguments in detail (step C, above).

What problem is the author trying to solve? Does his formulation of the problem rest on any assumptions, tacit or explicitly stated?

How is he treating the problem? What is his method of solution?

On what assumptions does the author base his arguments?

What assumptions are needed for his argument, even though not explicitly stated by him?

Is his argument valid? Is it sound?

How does each particular argument fit into the work as a whole? Is it necessary to the main argument?

If the author has made a mistake, is it an instructive one? How is it that he was led astray? Perhaps in formulating an answer to this last question, one will hit upon a general mistake, which is likely to be made in other contexts as well.

2. *Writing Philosophy*

Analytic philosophy is an activity that is pursued in the hope of achieving precision and clarity about the concepts, logical structure, methods, and objects of human knowledge. Thus, precision and clarity are minimal criteria of acceptability in philosophical writing. But precision and clarity, sad to say, are as hard to achieve as excellence in style. Whoever wishes to do philosophical analysis, therefore, must consciously endeavor to meet the standards that the discipline imposes.

As with other kinds of writing, the only way to learn to write philosophy is by making the attempt. One must write, subject the result to careful criticism, and then write again, bearing in mind the criticism. But it is not only others who can provide such beneficial criticism. On the contrary, the ability to read one's own writing with critical scrutiny is a major asset to writers of all sorts and a mark of successful writers in any field. Yet one can be usefully critical, of oneself or of others, only to the extent to which one has standards of criticism.

Everything that has been said above about reading philosophy is equally true when it is one's own philosophical writing that is being read. Thus, remarks about what to look for when reading philosophy provide some basis for self-criticism in writing philosophy. If one knows what to look for in the writing of others, then one can, insofar as it is possible to remain objective, evaluate one's own work. But the tendency is to read one's own writing with extraordinary sympathy—to overlook failings that would be immediately apparent in the writing of others. Thus, reading one's own philosophy critically is generally more difficult than reading the work of others.

Some progress in the effort to be objectively self-critical may result from explicit consideration of the nature of common failings in philosophical writing. Such consideration should, at least, alert the beginning writer of philosophy to specific dangers to which he is likely to fall victim. We shall, therefore, present in the remainder of this section a discussion of some characteristic weaknesses of beginning papers in philosophy. The material in the following two sections should be of some use in helping the writer to avoid those weaknesses.

A student's first writing in philosophy is commonly very unclear. This lack of clarity results from many factors, some of which can be explicitly isolated. Among the most common are:

A. The use of phrases and expressions which have no meaning, or no meaning that is clear in the context. Consider in this connection the phrase 'the *nearly infinite* value of a human life'. What does 'nearly infinite' mean—large but finite? Or actually infinite?

B. The use of equivocal terms or phrases (i.e., ambiguous terms or phrases) as if they were univocal. Consider: 'The *purpose* of this knife is to cut grapefruit'. Does 'purpose' in this sentence mean the purpose for which the knife was designed or the purpose for which it is used? It may be a knife designed specifically to cut grapefruit or it may be a bent steak knife that is used to cut grapefruit.

C. Reliance on unexplained metaphors or analogies. For example, 'The human mind is like a computer'. In what specific ways is it like a computer? Certainly not in being made of metal.

D. Reliance on jargon—that is, the use of phrases which have a familiar or authoritative ring but little content. Consider: 'Without absolute standards there can be no moral worth'. The phrase 'absolute standard' is a familiar one, but it is used in so many different ways that its meaning in this context is not clear.

More generally, papers in philosophy commonly suffer from a lack of substantial content. This lack is often due in part to one or more of the following mistakes:

A. Failure to take note of important relevant distinctions, e.g., failure to distinguish, in a paper about values, between what *is* and what *ought to be*.

B. Overemphasis of a single aspect of a problem—e.g., in a discussion of principles of education, speaking of man as an economic or intellectual being, without mentioning or justifying the restriction to these aspects of man.

C. Failure to formulate the problem at hand in a precise and clear way.

D. Failure to come to grips with a problem once it is formulated. This failing frequently results in papers which, while not containing assertions or arguments that are themselves objectionable, provide more wind than substance. Usually, assertions in papers of this type, if they are intelligible, are so vague and general that it is difficult to imagine how they could be doubted or why they need be said.

E. Failure to perceive the lack of precision in ordinary language. Just what, for example, does it mean to say, as people often do, that morality is objective? Is it objective because it is measurable by scientific observation, as the weight of a stone is, or what?

F. Failure to reread critically to insure both that one has said what he has meant to say and that one means what he has in fact said.

3. Use and Mention

In this section, as throughout this book, we have occasion to talk *about* words, to *mention* a word rather than to *use* it. The device of using single quotation marks to indicate that a word is being mentioned and not used is found frequently in philosophical writings and is deserving of attention here.

An author writing about Franklin Delano Roosevelt will have many occasions to mention the thirty-second President. He will mention Roosevelt, for example, in any sentence that is about Roosevelt; and he will mention the thirty-second President by using his name or some description that uniquely describes Roosevelt. In the preceding two sentences, Roosevelt has been mentioned six times, four times by using his name and twice by using a definite description, i.e., 'the thirty-second President'. A man and his name are quite different entities; one is an animal, the other an element of language. Sentences are composed of elements of a language; one could not use Roosevelt himself in a sentence any more than one could shake hands with Roosevelt's name.

Analogously, when one talks about a word or mentions a word in a sentence, one does so by using the name of that word in the sentence. But the name of a word is also a word; both are elements of language, both can be used in sentences, and thus they may easily be confused. The name of a word is formed by enclosing the word within *single* quotation marks. A name formed in this way refers to the *word* of which it is a name, just as Roosevelt's name refers to the man of whom it is a name. The name of a word does not refer to the object or objects referred to by the word of which it is a name. A word may not refer to any object, but its name always refers to the word, e.g., 'is' does not refer to any object, but 'is' refers to a word. Let us consider some further examples:

(1) Red is a color.
(2) 'Red' is a three-letter word.
(3) John is a boy.
(4) 'John' is a boy's name.

Each of these sentences is true, while the following sentences are false:

(5) Red is a three-letter word.
(6) 'Red' is a color.
(7) 'John' is a boy.
(8) John is a boy's name.

Sentence (5) is false because it states that a color is a word, while (6) is false because it states that a word is a color. (7) and (8) reveal a similar confusion of a name with the name of a name. Sometimes we may wish to refer to a word in a sentence; consider these examples:

(9) 'Red' in sentence (5) refers to a color.
(10) ' 'Red' ' in sentence (6) refers to a word.
(11) ' 'Red' ' appears in sentence (6), but 'red' does not.

Each of these sentences is true, but the following sentence is false because it states that a word which refers to a color refers to a word:

(12) 'Red' in sentence (5) refers to a word.

We may form the name of a sentence, a predicate, or a description in an analogous way. Consider:

(13) 'John believes it hailed yesterday' is an intensional sentence.

(14) 'is a Senator from California' is a predicate true of Senator Cranston.

(15) 'The Senator from California' fails to describe one and only one individual.

Notice that the following sentence is not even grammatically correct, because there is no subject of the verb 'is':

(16) John believes it hailed yesterday is an intensional sentence.

In sentence (10) we used the name of a name of a word. We form the name of a name just as we form the name of any other word, by enclosing the name in single quotation marks. Similarly we can form the name of a name of a name, etc., the limit to this procedure being one of intelligibility rather than one of logic.

4. Words to Watch

Words are used for various purposes. Some words that suffice for use in everyday communication do not suffice for philosophical discussions, perhaps because they are vague in their ordinary use. Or perhaps it is because it has been to the philosopher's interest to draw fine distinctions with which one is not concerned outside of philosophical study and that therefore are not reflected in words as they are ordinarily used. Below we shall mention some words and phrases that are best avoided in philosophical discussions and some that should be used only with considered caution.

Semantics is most commonly understood by philosophers as theory of meaning, encompassing questions about the sense and reference of words. As such, it is concerned with the relations between a sign (or word) and what the sign signifies (or means). Semantics in this sense may be contrasted with syntactics, which is concerned in part with formal relations between signs and with the rules by which signs may be combined to yield well-formed formulas (sentences) in a given language. There are indeed many *semantical questions,* including those problems concerning sentences, words, and meaning mentioned above in Chapters IV and V, as well as questions in the theory of truth and questions concerning the relations between a name and the object it names. But to say that something is "just a matter of semantics" or "just a question of semantics" can be misleading. We have seen in the previous discussion of philosophical analysis that definitions in accord with strict criteria may be a goal of some philosophical investigation. But to suppose that one can dismiss a philosophical problem by asserting that it is just a matter of definition or semantics is to miss the point of what a philosophical problem is, if such an assertion is intended to imply that the problem can be solved by arbitrarily defining certain terms. Arbitrary definitions will not solve any philosophical problem.

Whether it is sentences or propositions that can be true, a particular sentence or proposition is either true or false. To say that a sentence is *really true* is to say no more than that it is true. And to say that one sentence is *more true* or *closer to the truth* than another is often to engender confusion. If two sentences are both true, they are equally true. If both are false, then neither is true, nor is one more true than the other. If one sentence is true and another false, it may be appropriate to speak of the first as more true than the second, but this locution does not convey any more information about the sentences than is conveyed simply by saying that one is true and the other false. It may, of course, be that there is better evidence for one sentence than another or better reason to believe one than another. Instead of saying of such sentences that one is more true than the other, it is clearer to show that the evidence for the one is better than that for the other.

The words *'subjective'*, *'objective'*, *'relative'*, and *'absolute'* have often been used by philosophers. But no one of these terms has had only one use. It is safe to say that these words should be avoided as much as possible. Whenever something is said to be relative, one must also say to *what* it is relative. "What is right is relative" is not a complete assertion until one has said whether what is right is relative to a particular society, individual, or what; and how. When 'absolute' is used with the intention of conveying the idea 'not relative', the question "Not relative to what?" becomes relevant. Like 'relative' and 'absolute', the words 'subjective' and 'objective' have often been assumed to be opposite in meaning. But since none of these four words has either a clear meaning or a standardized use in philosophical discussions, this opposition is of no help in clarifying the meaning of any of these words. It is worth noting that 'subjective' need not be a pejorative adjective, nor 'objective' an adjective of commendation. Each of these words should be used only with an explanation of how and why it is being used. Often such an explanation suffices to make the point for which the word seemed useful.

The words discussed below are used clearly only when certain questions are answered about each particular use. Consider the assertion that two events or objects are *similar, alike,* or *different*. Such assertions are interesting only when it is said in what respects the things are similar or different, because no matter how different any two things are, there is some respect in which they are alike; and no matter how similar or alike two things are, they are different in some respect. For example, two sentences may be alike in both being extensional but different in their truth value; two objects may be without perceptible difference in color, size, and shape, and yet be in different places. Referring back to section 1 of Chapter III, you will see that analogous remarks are applicable to the word 'same'. We often say of one object that it is different from what it once was, that it has *changed* or is *changing*. Just as one needs to specify in what ways two different things are different, so must one say in what respects one and the same thing has changed or is different. The assertion that two objects or events are the same and yet different need not be contradictory, although it may be. Its meaning simply is not clear until it is indicated in what respect, or in relation to which properties, the objects are the same and different.

The words *'efficient'*, *'deficient'*, *'perfect'*, *'complete'*, and *'adequate'* similarly call for an answer to the questions "In what respects?" or "By what standards?" or "For what purposes?" Thus a knife may be efficient for cutting meat and inefficient for turning screws. A rose may be a perfect flower but an imperfect source of nourishment. A student's program of study may be adequate for a high school diploma but inadequate for college admission. And a cereal may be complete as a supply of vitamin requirements for a child but incomplete for an adolescent.

The words *'object'*, *'entity'*, and *'thing'* must be used with one caution in mind. None of these words provides a criterion for individuation; that is, one can know the meaning of the word 'thing' and still be unable to distinguish one thing from another. In contrast, if one knows the meaning of the word 'man', he can distinguish one man from another or count the number of men in a room. But suppose that one were asked to count the number of things or objects in a room in which there were ten men. He would not know whether to count each man's leg as an entity; he would not know whether to count men's arms as well as men's hands as things. Thus to say of anything that it is an entity or an object or a thing is to provide little or no information about it.

Words or sentences that have no clearly defined meaning or use may be said to be *vague*. The word 'absolute' is vague, as is the sentence 'There are no absolute standards of morality'. In contrast, an *ambiguous* word or sentence is one that has more than one meaning. 'Bridge' is an ambiguous word, and if Jones is a man who builds spans over water and wears false teeth, the sentence 'Jones's new bridge is poorly designed' is ambiguous. It is also said that a word or sentence is *meaningless*. Some philosophers have asserted that the sentence 'God exists' is meaningless because it is neither analytic nor confirmable by experience. Clearly such an assertion presupposes a standard of meaningfulness—namely, that any statement which is meaningful is either analytic or subject to empirical confirmation. So when a word or sentence is asserted to be meaningless, the question "by what criterion of meaningfulness?" is in order. Most frequently, the assertion that a sentence is meaningless is intended to indicate that the sentence has no content and conveys no information. Therefore, a meaningless sentence is neither true nor false; that is, it has no content on the basis of which its truth value could be determined.

Exercises

1. Illustrate the difference between use and mention.

2. Indicate the truth value of the following:
    (a) Blue has four letters.
    (b) 'Red' is a color.
    (c) John is a boy's name.
    (d) 'Red' has four letters.
    (e) Blue is a color.

3. Distinguish between vagueness and ambiguity.

4. What is wrong with the question 'How many things are there in this room?'

5. What is suspect about the following claim? 'Since men and apes are so much alike and porpoises are so unlike both, apes will exhibit a high degree of problem-solving ability whereas porpoises will not'.

IX

Divisions of Philosophy

1. Introduction

Philosophy is a broad field of study within which it is possible to delimit more specific areas of inquiry. Such divisions have been made traditionally on the basis of the nature of the questions considered in each area. In this chapter, we shall deal with the general content of the major areas of philosophy by indicating some problems illustrative of each area. But these problems we mention will hardly be exhaustive of the areas; rather, they are selected as typical. Moreover, it is a serious error to suppose that a question in philosophy falls neatly within one specialized area. In fact, there are many problems in philosophy that are of major concern to specialists in several areas. In such cases, one can think of the areas in philosophy as representing not so much various sets of questions but rather various points of view from which the questions are to be considered. Thus, it is rare indeed that real progress in one area of philosophy does not shed some light in other areas. And as one might expect, a mark of the importance of a problem in philosophy is the extent to which it permeates the various divisions within the field. The picture we will provide of the divisions of philosophy will thus be rough—but that is well, for the divisions are rough; and it would be a great mistake to consider them to be clearly delineated.

2. Theory of Value

A. ETHICS

We evaluate our own and others' actions; for example:

(1) Dr. Smith will do the *right* thing if he tells his patient the truth about his illness.
(2) I am *obligated* to repay the money I borrowed from Bill.

Evaluations can also be made of kinds of actions; for example:

(3) It is always *right* to tell the truth.
(4) Repaying debts is *obligatory*.

And evaluations can be made of people as agents, i.e., persons who act; for example:

(5) Smith did not have to accept the offer; he was *free* to do as he chose.
(6) Jones was *worthy of praise* for saving Brown from drowning.

Speaking generally, we may say that each of these examples is an assertion about moral value. Ethics is, in part, an investigation into the nature of moral judgment and moral reasoning. Typical of the questions that fall within the scope of ethics is the following: If a man says that an act is right, is he just saying something about himself—for example, that he approves of the act; or is he saying something about the property rightness, which the act has independently of his attitude? Closely linked with this question is the question of what facts about the act one could cite as evidence for the correctness of judgments of the kinds exemplified above by (1) to (6). If such a judgment is only a report of the feelings of the judge toward the act, is any evidence about the act relevant to determining the truth value of the judgment?

Questions in ethics then are not specific questions about whether a particular act is right or wrong; ethics is to be distinguished from moralizing or casuistry. Ethical arguments are not exhortations to some course of action. It is true that philosophers writing in ethics have not always avoided giving moral advice. But ethical philosophers, qua philosophers, discuss instead the *nature of reasoning* about moral matters and propose criteria on the basis of which such reasoning is to be evaluated.

What distinguishes good from bad reasons offered in favor of moral judgments? One sometimes supports a particular judgment [for example (1) above] by appeal to a general principle [for example (3) above]. But philosophers have been concerned to determine in just what way general principles do support particular claims. Imagine a disagreement between Mr. Black and Mr. White. Black argues that (1) is a correct judgment because the doctor's telling his patient the truth is a particular instance of the kind of action mentioned in (3). White denies that (1) is correct; he cites another general principle, that a doctor is obliged to do whatever is possible to improve his patient's condition. White asserts that this patient's condition would be worsened by his knowledge of the severity of his condition and therefore that for Dr. Smith to tell the patient the truth must be wrong because to do so is to violate the doctor's obligation to improve his patient's health.

This supposed disagreement raises several problems that have concerned ethical philosophers. First we see that the general principles to which White and Black appeal support conflicting judgments about the moral value of a particular act. Perhaps we must evaluate the general principles before we can judge the cogency of the arguments presented. One may ask whether there can be evidence for general principles at all; perhaps we should evaluate a principle by inquiring into the acceptability of the particular judgments it supports. But if we argue that general principles support particular judgments and that acceptability of a general principle is to be decided on the basis of the judgments it supports, our argument seems to be circular.

In this dispute, White cited a fact about the patient's condition, the fact that the patient's condition would deteriorate if he learned of the severity of his illness. Philosophers have often discussed the role that facts such as this, which do not themselves involve value judgments, play in moral reasoning. Is it always possible to distinguish descriptive or factual claims from evaluative claims? How can factual evidence ever be relevant to moral judgments?

It has often been argued that unless one understands the meaning of such terms as 'right', 'obligatory', 'free', and 'responsible', which are used in ethical judgments, one cannot begin to answer other questions in ethics. Thus some writers in ethics have attempted to define or explicate 'right' or the rightness of an action either in terms of its consequences or in terms of the motives from which it was done. Other writers have argued that no noncircular definition is possible. Still others have argued that such terms as 'right' have no meaning but rather are used simply to express approval.

Inquiry into the meaning of expressions used in ethical judgments is relevant to the question of what is evidence for a moral judgment. If we believe that 'right' means 'done from altruistic motives', then whatever is evidence that an act was done from altruistic motives is at the same time evidence that the act was right. The question of evidence is central to the problem of evaluating a person's moral reasoning or of adjudicating between the disputants in an argument concerning matters of value.

Discussion of the rightness or wrongness of actions has been closely connected with discussions of the moral worth of agents. Philosophers have been concerned to discuss what reasons are relevant to the evaluation of a person as, for example, praiseworthy or blameworthy for an action. Problems concerning the logical relations between a person's being free and his being responsible and between his being responsible and his being worthy of praise or blame have been considered throughout the history of ethical philosophy.

B. AESTHETICS

Not all evaluations are of actions; not all value is ethical value. We judge one painting to be better than another, evaluate the rhythm of a poem, criticize the form of a sculpture. One studies such evaluations in aesthetics, but judgments about beauty are not limited to works of art. They may apply as well to natural objects and events, such as mountains and sunsets. Thus, aesthetics is not limited to the study of evaluations of artifacts. In fact, one of the questions that interests aestheticians is whether or not there is any way to delimit the range of objects that can have aesthetic value.

Analogously to questioning in ethics, one may ask

whether or not the beauty of an object can be defined in terms of some or all of the object's descriptive properties or qualities. Does the subject matter of a work of art contribute to its aesthetic value? For example, if kindness is better than cruelty, is a poem praising kindness better than one praising cruelty?

The question also arises whether there can be any basis for criticizing someone's judgment that a painting or poem is beautiful. Is such a judgment merely an expression of taste? Or do aesthetic judgments, like those in science, stand in need of justification? If so, how can they be defended?

Aesthetics is not art criticism; aestheticians are not concerned to evaluate particular works of art or to advise artists how to create better works of art. Rather, aestheticians have typically been concerned with such questions as whether there is an aesthetic attitude, a particular way in which one must regard an object, in order to appreciate its aesthetic value or beauty. Writers in aesthetics have proposed and criticized criteria for the evaluation of aesthetic judgments; they have proposed and criticized general principles that might support particular judgments; finally, they have often discussed whether any such criteria are even possible.

C. GENERAL VALUE THEORY

Some philosophers have argued that we would better understand both ethical and aesthetic judgments if we could view such judgments in the wider context of evaluation in general. Besides evaluating men and their actions and works of art, we also evaluate such diverse things as tools, food, athletes, mechanical skills, amusements, techniques, etc. And we engage in such different—but related

—activities as grading, appreciating, praising, recommending, instituting, legislating, and criticizing. Many of these objects of evaluation and ways of evaluating are significantly different from the topics traditionally treated under the heading of ethics or aesthetics.

Indeed, it may be the case that by concentrating on the moral and the beautiful we have distorted both the importance and the peculiar role of aesthetic and ethical judgments and have failed to notice important similarities between, for example, good men and good typewriters or between morally good actions and skillful performances. But, be that as it may, these other modes of evaluation are philosophically important and interesting in their own right if for no other reason than that they make up the bulk of our day-to-day evaluative judgments.

3. Epistemology

There are many things which we claim to know—for example: (1) that all men are animals, (2) that Lassie is a collie, (3) that cigarette smoking is causally related to lung cancer, and (4) that every event has a cause. We are not usually called upon to justify our claims to knowledge. But if someone were to assert that there were green men living on Mars, we might well ask him how he knew or what his evidence was. If he replied that he knew because he had seen green Martians in his crystal ball, we would question both the acceptability of his evidence and the truth of his original assertion.

Epistemology is an inquiry into the nature of knowledge. But the epistemologist is not asking what the evidence is for *particular* knowledge claims. Rather, part of the inquiry of epistemology is directed toward ascertaining what *kind* of evidence is relevant to a particular *kind* of knowledge claim. For example, the statement that no crystal ball vision is evidence relevant to an empirical claim is an epistemological assertion. It was the observation that there are different kinds of claims to knowledge, requiring different sorts of evidence that led philosophers to draw the distinctions discussed above (Chapter VI) between analytic and synthetic sentences and between *a priori* and *a posteriori* knowledge.

In the course of investigating the relation between the evidence for an assertion and the assertion itself, the epistemologist may ask whether the evidence must be known with certainty. For example, does the fact that we may sometimes be misled by our senses invalidate perception as a source of evidence? Since the evidence for some claims [such as (2) above] must be at least in part perceptual, if one argues that perception is not a reliable source of evidence, he thereby argues that no empirical statement like (2) can ever be known to be true. And, in so arguing, he would be offering a partial answer to one epistemological question—what sorts of things can we know?

We have suggested that the task of the epistemologist differs from that of the scientist. Consider, as illustrative of the point, the question of how or whether we are able to see colors. The physicist or physiologist may take this question to be equivalent to the question of how we make color discriminations. He may then study physical conditions of sight such as illumination, eye structure, and neurological connections between the eye and the brain. The philosopher, on the other hand, may argue that we do not see colors at all. What we see, he may claim, are colored objects. If A sees X, then X appears some way to A. But colors don't appear any way to anyone. Objects can appear red, but how does red appear? Does it ever look orange? Objects can appear different than they are, but how can colors do this? Thus, the philosopher's approach includes conceptual analysis of what it means to say that someone sees something.

Another problem typical of epistemological inquiry concerns the status of induction as a source of evidence for claims to knowledge.

Inductive arguments begin with particular observation statements or a statement summarizing particular observations; they have as conclusions either (1) a general statement, not all of whose particular instances are known, or (2) a particular statement about an as yet unknown state of affairs. An example of (1) is:

> All Presidents of the United States thus far have been men.
> (Therefore) All Presidents of the United States will be men.

And an example of (2) is:

> All Presidents of the United States thus far have been men.
> (Therefore) The next President of the United States will be a man.

Neither of these arguments is deductively valid; it is logically possible that the next President of the United States will be a woman, even though the above premise is true.

Although logicians have criteria for the admissibility of rules of deductive inference as well as a complete and sound set of rules that satisfy these criteria, no such criteria or set of rules exist for inductive arguments. And because it is always logically possible that the conclusion of an inductive argument may be false even though its premises are true, some philosophers have argued that induction does not provide an acceptable source of evidence, that the mere fact that some proposition is the conclusion of an inductive argument cannot constitute sufficient reason for a claim to know that that proposition is true. The philosophical discussion of induction resembles the discussion of the status of perceptual evidence in that it is a general inquiry into what, if anything, constitutes good evidence for a particular type of claim.

Argument by analogy is sometimes considered a type of inductive argument. Attention has been directed toward the question of the validity of this kind of argument because it has seemed a method by which we might justify claims of knowledge about others' minds—for example, about what another person believes. We cannot observe another's mind, but we can observe his actions. Suppose Mr. Smith is acting exactly as I do when I believe that it is going to rain today. When I act as he is now acting, I do so because I believe it will rain today. I can observe these likenesses in behavior and then conclude that we are alike in beliefs as well, i.e., that he believes it is going to rain today. Yet there is always the logical possibility that he acts as he does because he holds a belief different from mine, e.g., that taking an umbrella will prevent rain. In an argument by analogy, it is observed that certain of the properties of some things are the same, in this case that Smith is acting as I act when I believe it will rain. On the basis of the observed similarities, it is concluded that the things are also alike in some unobserved respects, in this case that we are alike in our belief that it will rain.

Not all epistemological questions are directly concerned with the relation between evidence and a proposition that

someone claims to know. We claim to know not only propositions but how to do things—how to swim, spell, or play
chess. And we claim to know people and places, to know
Chief Justice Warren or San Francisco. Philosophers have
discussed whether there is any common factor present in
all cases of knowing—perhaps a state of mind or the ability to perform in a certain way. The question of what counts
as evidence when one claims to know how to swim or to
know San Francisco has also been discussed, along with
the question of the relation between evidence for these
claims and evidence for the truth of propositions.

4. Metaphysics

We have said that many questions are studied from the
standpoint of one or another specialized area of philosophy
and that it is impossible to give more than a rough delinea-
tion of the divisions within philosophy. Nowhere is it more
difficult to isolate an area by reference to its problems than
in metaphysics. One reason for this difficulty is that throughout the history of philosophy many problems have at one
time been called metaphysical and at other times been denied that appellation. Some philosophers, distressed by the
sort of speculation that has been called metaphysics, have
denied that the problems with which they were concerned
were metaphysical ones. Others have argued that these
philosophers were nevertheless still dealing with traditional
problems of metaphysics and that no renaming of a problem would change its nature. With these difficulties in
mind, let us make some general remarks about some problems that have most usually been called metaphysical and
about the status of the propositions of metaphysics.

Metaphysics is concerned with the way in which we

think about the world. Some metaphysicians have held that the concepts basic to our thought could not be other than they are. They have gone on to inquire into which concepts must be presupposed by the structure of our thought. We distinguish individuals—the sorts of things that possess properties—from the properties they possess. This distinction, often referred to as that between particulars and universals, has been cited as an example of a distinction fundamental to our way of thinking; and it has brought forth many questions in metaphysics. For example, what are the criteria by which we individuate particulars, i.e., distinguish one particular object from another? On what grounds do we say that the butterfly that emerges from a cocoon is one and the same animal as the caterpillar that spun the cocoon? Do the criteria for individuating people imply that there are some essential properties that an object must possess in order to be a person? Suppose, for example, that a person loses all reasoning power; is what remains still a person? Or are there some changes a person could undergo, after which what remains would no longer be a person?

Regarding universals, it has been long debated whether or not they exist independently of their being manifested in particulars. Could there, for example, be whiteness if there were no white objects? Further, one may ask how universals can be individuated one from another. Can one explain the difference between redness and greenness with no reference to red or green particulars?

Not all metaphysicians have accepted the way in which we normally think about the world as inevitable or even correct. Some have suggested that we alter the structure of our thought, arguing, for example, that the world we perceive through our senses is but an appearance of some transcendent reality. Many have gone on to consider the nature of this supposed reality, suggesting that it consists of some sort of mind or collection of ideas, rather than of physical matter.

Such questions, about just what it is that actually exists, are called *ontological* questions. Thus the question of whether universals exist independently of the particulars that instantiate them is an ontological question. Some philosophers have argued that universals do exist but in a different sense of the word 'exist' from that in which particulars are said to exist. Whether the word 'exist' is genuinely equivocal in such a way is open to question.

The question of just what kinds of things exist is one of importance to many areas of philosophy, and thus philosophers have studied in detail the consequences of various answers. If matter is held to be the only kind of thing that exists and if, in addition, matter is subject to causal laws, can there be freedom of the will? The answer to this question is of importance, for example, in moral and legal philosophy, where questions of responsibility arise. On the other hand, if one is an idealist, i.e., if one holds that ideas alone exist, various epistemological questions arise at once. For instance, how can sensory experience be evidence for a proposition about ideas?

It is often difficult to know what would count as evidence for a metaphysical claim. The proposition that universals exist independently of particulars would usually be regarded as synthetic. Yet it seems totally unsusceptible of an *a posteriori* proof. In general, metaphysical claims are synthetic but admit only of an *a priori* proof. As you have read in Chapter VI, many philosophers deny that there can be any *a priori* proof of a synthetic statement. Therefore, they question whether metaphysical statements can ever be known to be true. In discussions of the status of metaphysical propositions and the knowledge we can have of them, the distinction between metaphysics and epistemology is difficult, if not impossible, to draw. Similarly, questions of freedom and determinism bring ethics and metaphysics together; and there is a close connection between logic and metaphysics. For in the discussion of the predicate calculus, it was pointed out that the logician must specify the range of his variables, the types of entities for which the variables stand. But what types of entities there are, i.e., what types of things the variables can stand for, is surely a metaphysical question.

Finally, metaphysics is often inseparable from the philosophy of language. Some metaphysicians have claimed that the syntactic and semantic structure of our language blinds us to certain features of reality while overemphasizing other features, and they have recommended linguistic changes designed to meet these difficulties. Others have claimed that such wholesale changes lead to incoherence.

5. *Logic*

Logic is a philosophical study of certain properties of human reasoning. A psychologist might be interested in how people reason; common forms of incorrect reasoning would be as interesting to him as common forms of correct reasoning. But the logician's concern is with an analysis of the structure of correct reasoning. The rules of inference in a system of logic are based on principles of human reasoning but with the condition that these rules preserve validity—that is, that from true premises they allow the inference only of a true conclusion.

It was pointed out in Chapter I that the validity of an argument depends only on its form. Systems of symbolic logic, with a specified vocabulary and precise rules for forming sentences and drawing inferences, are designed to display the form of an argument as clearly as possible. We may regard a system of symbolic logic as a language, an artificial language developed to avoid whenever possible the vagueness and ambiguity inherent in a natural language, such as English or French. When a sentence is translated from English into symbolic notation, it often loses some of the nuances it had in English, but, in return for this loss, its logical form is made clear and precise if the translation is an adequate one. A logician, then, may be concerned with the criteria which can be cited to support the claim that one symbolization of a given English sentence is better than another. The relations between a formal and a natural language raise questions that concern the logician as well as the philosopher of language. For example, in a symbolization, just how much of the meaning of a sentence may be sacrificed in the name of precision? Sometimes such questions lead to a reformulation of the system of logic in an attempt to incorporate into it some of the important features of natural language formerly left out of account.

Logicians are also concerned with discovering what properties a system of symbolic logic possesses—e.g., whether it is complete and sound. To say that such a system is complete is to say that *all* the arguments which are semantically valid (which are such that it must be that if premises are true, then the conclusion is true) can be shown to be syntactically valid (i.e., the conclusion can be derived from the premises within the rules of the system). To say the system is sound is to say that *only* semantically valid inferences are allowed by the rules.

For further insight into the study of logic, the reader

should refer to Chapters I and II and should also see section 6 (below) on philosophy of mathematics.

6. *Philosophy of Mathematics*

Like philosophers of science and of history, philosophers of mathematics have been concerned with both the methods and the subject matter of the discipline that they study. Most people achieve some proficiency in elementary mathematics without ever questioning the nature of numbers themselves. The philosopher of mathematics considers such questions, asking whether numbers are objects, concepts, properties of sets of objects, or perhaps sets. Further, the philosopher asks what sort of evidence, if any, is relevant to mathematical assertions. A child may have his first acquaintance with numbers by being shown one orange, then two, then three. But this does not show that arithmetical truths are empirical. Rather, one can argue that mathematical propositions are analytic, since it seems that they can be proven by logical and set-theoretical considerations alone. But if we argue that mathematical propositions are analytic and hence have no extralogical content, we are then faced with the problem of accounting for the apparent relevance of mathematics to the empirical world.

On the other hand, if we hold that mathematical truths are synthetic, we must account for their apparent necessity —for the apparent incoherence inherent in the denial of a truth of mathematics.

Philosophers of mathematics have inquired into the notion of a set, investigating the consistency of intuitive set theory and seeking to determine whether set theory can be reduced to logic. The relation between numbers and sets is also a matter for investigation. Is it possible, for example, to define numbers in terms of sets? If so, what is to be gained by so doing?

Some of these questions lead us to ask just what would constitute good reasons for believing that mathematical propositions are in fact either analytic or synthetic. Such a question has to do with what constitutes a proof *about* mathematics. But we can also ask what constitutes a proof *within* mathematics. And the question of what constitutes such a proof is as much a question of logic as of philosophy of mathematics. Thus, for this among other reasons, the philosophy of mathematics is inseparable from the study of formal logic.

7. *Philosophy of Science*

There are many notions used in science that the scientist, in his capacity as a scientist, does not usually analyze. There are many presuppositions that he cannot be expected either to make explicit or to justify. Nor does the scientist typically investigate the nature of scientific method, of scientific theory, or of scientific knowledge and the propositions of science. The philosopher of science, however, may be expected to undertake just such tasks as these.

It is obvious that a great deal of material is common to epistemology and the philosophy of science. Among the scientist's presuppositions must surely be some belief in the possibility of empirical knowledge. And any discussion of the nature of a scientific theory will include the question of confirmation and the notions of induction and probability.

Currently, much discussion in the philosophy of science centers around the problems of explanation and prediction. In order for one to be able to explain a particular phenomenon, must a statement of its occurrence be capable of being deduced from causal laws and from some statements about causal conditions? Is an explanation of this deductive form typical of scientific explanations? Is there only one logical form for an acceptable explanation? What lies behind our conviction that it is a better explanation of a baby's having blue eyes that his parents have blue eyes than that his mother ate blueberries during her pregnancy? Or, in general, why is science preferable to augury? Similar questions may be asked about predictions. What must be the logical form of a prediction if it is to be justified? And what is the relation between the form of an explanation and that of a prediction?

Questions about explanation and prediction are among the many that give rise to questions about causality. What does it mean when a doctor says that an antibiotic injection can have many different effects? An introduction to the kind of interest a philosopher may have in this question is presented in Chapter VII, above. Philosophers have been interested in what it means to say that a particular event A caused another event B. Does such an assertion imply that there is a general law about events like A causing events like B? Questions like this present a natural introduction to an inquiry into the nature of scientific laws. One may ask why some general statements are laws—for example, Mendel's laws of genetics—while other true general statements are not—for example, 'All children's shoes purchased in California in 1962 cost more than $.05 per pair when new.'

What is the justification for theories that bear no obvious relation to everyday experience and for the introduction of such terms as 'atom', 'proton', 'neutron', and 'electron'? What is the relation between theories involving concepts such as these and the experimental results that these theories purport to explain? And what, if any, are the implications of such theories for philosophical inquiry generally? For example, philosophers have often discussed the concept of time and have used and discussed the notion of simultaneity. What relevance has Einstein's theory of time to such a discussion? Or again, Heisenberg's uncertainty principle entails that in some respects the future cannot be predicted even on the basis of the best possible information about the past and present. Is this principle relevant to the philosopher's discussion of determinism and free will? Or is the will that philosophers have discussed something quite independent of protons, neutrons, and the like? In general we may say that it has been a philosophical question whether science and philosophy constitute different methods of studying the same subject matter or whether the subject matters of the two fields are quite independent of each other.

It has often been assumed that factual claims are more easily verified than value claims, that only factual claims have a place in science, and that the factual results of an experiment are brought into question if they depend on value judgments. Philosophers of science have questioned these assumptions; they have asked whether a scientist, in his role as scientist, makes value judgments and, if so, what effects these judgments have on the status of his experimental results. Is the scientist making a value judgment when he takes something to be a crucial experiment, when he decides that the results of one experiment are to be considered while those of another are to be discarded? If there is any one method which is *the* scientific method, is there any place in such a method for value judgments?

8. Philosophy of Language

We use language to communicate with one another; our being able to do so seems to presuppose that at least some of the words in our language have meanings which we understand and that our understanding is quite similar. But just what is the meaning of a word? And how does a word come to have the meaning it has? These are two general questions with which the philosophy of language is concerned.

In discussing ethics, we noted that it was not concerned with evaluating particular acts and, similarly, that epistemology was not concerned with compiling evidence for particular claims. An analogous disclaimer is in order for philosophy of language: In general, it is not the task of a philosopher investigating language to discover the meanings of particular words but rather to inquire into the relations among a word, its sense, its reference, the language in which it is a word, the users of that language, and the actions they can perform using language. In the course of this inquiry, philosophers may well attempt to analyze some terms that are essential in the philosophical study of language, e.g., 'meaning', 'truth', and 'synonymy'.

One of the basic facts about language is that it is possible to understand a sentence we have never seen before if we understand the words used to make up the sentence. So philosophers of language have been concerned to investigate the way in which the meaning of words contributes to the meaning of those sentences in which the words are used. In the course of this inquiry, investigation has been made into the logical form of sentences of different kinds— intensional and extensional, for example—in order to clarify the differences in the way words contribute to the meaning of sentences.

The topics discussed in Chapter IV are illustrative of problems in philosophy of language. What is the relation between the sense of a word and its reference? Is the meaning of a word nothing more than its sense and its reference, or are the images a word brings to mind part of its meaning? Some words do not, as far as we know, refer to anything in the world—for example, 'Pegasus', 'unicorn', 'centaur'. If the reference of a word is part of its meaning, how can we account for the fact that these words can be used in meaningful sentences? We have spoken of the *use* of words in sentences; philosophers have often discussed the relation between the use of a word and its meaning. An introduction to this discussion is presented in Chapter VII.

A major endeavor in the philosophy of language has been the search for a formal definition of truth, which neither leads to contradictions nor conflicts with our strong intuition that any sentence Φ is true if and only if the state of affairs described by Φ is the case. And it is as much in the philosophy of language as in epistemology that the dispute (noted in Chapter VI) as to whether or not the analytic-synthetic distinction is tenable has been waged.

The emphasis in recent years on logic and the analytic method of philosophy has no doubt stimulated interest in the problems of philosophy of language. Further, recent work in empirical linguistics, including the theory of transformational grammars, has increased philosophical inquiry directed at criticizing and describing the basic assumptions and methods of linguistic science and at applying the insights of linguists, where possible, to traditional philosophical problems. But like questions in other areas of philosophy, many of those in philosophy of language—such as "What is the meaning of 'truth'?"—have been discussed since the time of Plato and Aristotle.

9. *Philosophy of Mind*

Philosophy of mind, as a separate area of philosophical inquiry, has not played as prominent a role in the history of philosophy as ethics or epistemology. But this is not to say that the problems in this area have only recently come to be discussed. Inquiry into the nature of intentional action, desire, and motivation is present throughout the history of philosophy.

In discussing ethics, we noted that some philosophers have attempted to define the rightness of an action in terms of the motives from which the agent acted. To talk about a person's motives, intentions, desires, or beliefs is to talk about something mental or psychological. In order to gain some insight into the nature of these mental phenomena, philosophers have investigated the logical structure of the sentences used to describe motives, beliefs, and the like. Typically, such sentences are intensional (see Chapter V). Some philosophers of mind feel that intensionality is the most distinctive feature of discourse about psychological phenomena, and they have devoted their energies to a detailed study of the logical properties of intensional sentences.

The analysis of the concept of belief is another important problem in this area. Is what a person says about his beliefs to be taken as conclusive evidence of what he believes? The familiar saying that actions speak louder than words finds an analogue in the philosophical argument that what a person does must be taken as the final evidence of what he believes. Others have argued that it is not enough to say that a person's actions are *evidence* of his beliefs (or of his desires or intentions), rather that these mental notions have no meaning except that which can be defined in terms of a person's behavior or his physical responses to stimuli. Such problems of the relation of mind to body, of the mental to the physical, have played an important role in philosophy, particularly since Descartes.

Closely related to the concepts we have been discussing (e.g., motive, desire, etc.) is the concept of intentional action. So much philosophical inquiry has been focused on this concept in recent years that it would not be amiss to treat "philosophy of action" as a separate field. But to do so would be to de-emphasize the close connection between the problems involved in the analysis of action and other problems in the philosophy of mind.

What is the nature of action? How, for example, can the things a person does be distinguished from the things that happen to him? What is the relation between an action's being intentional and its being voluntary? And further, what is the distinction between a man's *deciding* to do something and his *predicting* that he will do it? All these are questions arising from the attempt to analyze the concept of action.

In addition, philosophers of mind have attempted to clarify the distinction between a person's *reasons* for acting as he does and the *causes* of his action. Are the beliefs, desires, and motives of a person reasons for his actions, or causes of them, or both?

It may seem difficult to distinguish the philosopher's task from the psychologist's. But the philosopher is not an empirical scientist. The relations he seeks among the concepts we have referred to are not connections one could discover in a laboratory. The philosopher seeks to make an analysis of such concepts as believing, desiring, and intending that will make clear the logical relations between them. For example, most philosophers hold that it is a logical presupposition of a person's intending to do something that he believes it to be possible for him to do it. The philosopher's evidence is not that people usually, or even always, believe that they can do what they intend to do. Rather, his evidence comes from an analysis of the concepts. His claim is that part of what it *means* to intend to do something is that one believes one can do it.

10. *Philosophy of History*

The philosopher of history studies history in much the same way as the philosopher of science studies science. He may ask just what history is, e.g., whether it is essential to history that historians interpret past events or attempt to discover patterns in history. Historians typically attempt to *explain* events and people's actions, and historical explanations have received as much attention from philosophers as have scientific explanations. Are historical explanations *causal* explanations? Are the requirements for an acceptable explanation in history different from those in science? The objects of historical study are primarily human actions and events as they influence and affect people; does this fact influence the kind of explanation that is appropriate? Does an explanation that gives the reasons for a person's action also give the causes? Is it a sufficient explanation for a person's action to give his reasons? What role does the notion of "law" play in history? Are there historical laws at all? Do the criteria for a law in history differ from those in science; could it be an historical law that a hungry people is a people bent on revolution?

A philosopher may also investigate the role that historical evidence plays in predictions. Does the logical form of the prediction of an event in the history of man parallel the logical form of a scientific prediction? There seem to be many ways in which the method of historians differs from that of scientists. To ask what history is is to ask in part whether history is a science. Do the differences between history and science cast doubt on the validity of history as a source of knowledge, or are the differences simply a product of different subject matter?

The question of evidence or good reasons recurs throughout philosophy, and philosophy of history is no exception. Historians often offer theories of history to account for the past, theories that may, for example, purport to show a pattern in past events. If two such theories conflict, what would constitute evidence in favor of either? Does the past itself provide evidence? Events in the past are in principle unobservable; they have already occurred. The philosopher of history shares with the epistemologist an interest in how or whether it is possible to have knowledge of the past. Does memory provide us with evidence about the past, or does the fact that one can believe he remembers something which did not actually occur invalidate evidence from memory?

11. Philosophy of Religion

Philosophy of religion is not theology nor is it a body of religious beliefs, rather it is a critical investigation of the meaning and justification of religious statements. Just as the philosopher may ask what constitutes scientific evidence, he may also ask what constitutes evidence for religious belief. While it is generally agreed, however, that scientific knowledge must be justified by appeal to evidence, it has been asked not only whether there *can* be evidence for religious propositions but also whether such propositions stand in need of supporting evidence.

Philosophers have inquired into just what kind of propositions the propositions of religion are. If they purport to give information about the world, they are not analytic. But if they are synthetic, on what grounds is one to confirm or deny them? Can revelation be a source of evidence? A distinction has often been made between revealed theology, by which this question is answered affirmatively, and rational or natural theology. Natural theology begins with evidence from the world or nature as we find it; it is said to be rational because its method is that of argument from purported facts about the world to claims about the existence and the nature of a divine being. If this distinction is correctly drawn, is there any reason to hold that one of these kinds of belief is better justified than the other?

Since the Middle Ages, when many philosophers were theologians as well, part of the philosophy of religion has been concerned with purported proofs for the existence of God. Are any proofs possible? The so-called ontological argument purports to deduce that God exists, not from empirical facts, but merely from an analysis of the concept of God. Many other arguments for the existence of God may be offered as well: An argument from design may be based on the claim that God must exist in order to account for the order in the universe. In giving a causal argument, one may hold that since everything that exists must have a cause, and the universe exists, then something must be the cause of the universe; and only God could be the cause of the universe. Finally, one may offer a moral argument to show that only in terms of God's existence can we explain moral values. But each of these arguments is open to serious objections of various sorts. Thus the philosopher of religion may ask whether these arguments can be defended against the objections, modified so as to avoid them, or supplanted by new arguments that are not open to objection.

The question of whether God exists or not is closely related to the question of the nature or attributes of God. If we merely assert that God exists but refuse to attempt to describe His nature, then the assertion of existence can be of no real interest. But if we attempt to describe His nature, then a host of new problems arises. If, for example, God is said to be omniscient, omnipotent, and benevolent, then the existence of evil poses a major difficulty. If God is omniscient, He knows about evil; if He is omnipotent, He can eliminate it; if He is benevolent, He opposes evil. Yet evil exists; God must therefore lack one of these three properties of omnipotence, omniscience, and benevolence. Such problems are typical of those in the philosophy of religion.

Not all philosophers, of course, have been concerned with statements about a god within the Judaeo-Christian tradition. Some have argued that while man can prove the existence of a god, it is one that differs significantly from the God of Western tradition. Others claim to be able to prove that no god exists; still others deny the meaningfulness of all claims about the existence of any being who cannot be verified empirically.

12. *Political Philosophy and Philosophy of Law*

Political philosophy consists essentially of inquiry into the relationship between individuals in a governed society and the government of that society. Unlike much of political science, it is not especially concerned with the description and analysis of existing governments. Rather, it is mainly concerned with examining the reasons for having any government at all and considering, in the light of those reasons, the justifiability of various features that governments may have. Thus, the political philosopher is likely to ask what general form the political organization of society should take. In seeking to answer this question, he will be faced with the task of considering the nature of man and the functions and purposes of social organization. Thomas Hobbes, for example, begins his treatise on political philosophy, *Leviathan,* with a discussion of the nature of man, arguing that in the absence of political organization life is "solitary, poor, nasty, brutish, and short" and that it is the function of political organization to provide men with a way of "getting themselves out from that miserable condition." He then goes on to consider, in the light of these views, what form the political organization of society should take.

Once a view of the nature of man and the function of political organization has been accepted, the question of the proper form of government involves many other philosophically interesting issues. What, for example, is the proper relation between law and morality? Some have argued that the body of laws in a society must reflect the moral attitudes which predominate in that society. Others hold that morality is essentially outside the law and that consequently it is inappropriate for legislation to be concerned with matters of morality at all. Rather, they argue, law results from an attempt by organized society to limit individual or group freedom, only insofar as its unrestricted exercise would injure individuals or groups within the society.

A related question, which is equally basic, concerns the procedure within the state for establishing and changing laws. When an individual is a member of a governed society, he is, it seems, committed to abide by its laws. What, then, are the rights and obligations of the citizen who considers a law to be unjustifiable? One can argue, for example, that it was wrong for citizens of Nazi Germany to obey Hitler's genocidal laws. But on what grounds was it wrong? Is it because obedience to those laws was a violation of some natural law? Such is the view that some philosophers have held. But then the question of the possibility of natural law must be considered, and new problems arise when we ask how natural laws, if there can be any, are discoverable.

Such questions about the nature and function of political organization are obviously inseparable from questions about the nature and function of laws. Hence there can be no complete division between political philosophy and philosophy of law. There are differences nonetheless. Philosophy of law, for example, is concerned to a large degree with philosophical issues connected with particular bodies of law or with the concept of law within a particular legal tradition. Thus, most philosophers of law in English-speaking countries are concerned with those questions that relate especially to the Anglo-American legal tradition.

Many of these questions are closely connected with problems in ethics, particularly those concerning the responsibility of agents. Systems of law as we know them rely on the notion of an agent's being responsible for his action. This is clearly revealed by the fact that we regard as relevant to the guilt of an accused person testimony as to whether or not he was under compulsion to act as he did. Two sets of questions naturally arise at this point. First, what does it mean to say that a person is or is not responsible? Is there, for instance, a difference between moral and legal responsibility? If so, what is the relationship between them? If not, how can we account for our conviction that justice and legality can sometimes fail to coincide?

Second, in what way does a person's lack of responsibility excuse him from blame or guilt, assuming that he did in fact perform the action in question? Such a question leads naturally to consideration of causality. For if we are to consider the consequences of an action in evaluating it, we must first be able to tell when a person's action is the cause of a subsequent event.

Further questions in philosophy of law also raise issues in other areas of philosophy. If, for example, we wish to hold that certain promises become binding contracts, we must be able to decide what is involved in the making of a promise. But what constitutes promising is a question in ethics and philosophy of language. And if we wish to count the intentions and motives of an agent as relevant in evaluating his action, this will lead us to consider what constitutes evidence about the mental state of another, what is involved in performing an act voluntarily, and what the connection is between freedom of the will and responsibility. These are paradigmatic questions of epistemology, philosophy of mind, and ethics.

13. History of Philosophy

The distinctions we have thus far suggested within the body of philosophy have been based on typical questions from each area. However, one may also regard philosophy through its chronological development, in the study of the history of philosophy. It is difficult to say exactly what constitutes an historical study of philosophy. If, for example, one were to study what philosophers during the seventeenth and eighteenth centuries wrote about epistemological questions, he would soon become involved in criticism and evaluation—that is, in epistemological inquiry. Yet he is also engaged in an historical study. And any purported epistemological study that does not take cognizance of the writings of past philosophers is simply not a thorough study. The problems of philosophy have not changed as much as, for instance, those of science; therefore, attention to past writings is not peripheral to contemporary philosophy, as it often is to contemporary science. In this sense, there is always reason for attention to history in philosophy.

One approach to an historical study of philosophy is, as we have mentioned above, to study those writings from a particular period of time that are concerned with selected problems. But many other approaches are possible. One can also study the writings of some one philosopher about many problems. In so doing, one may be interested in the effect that the philosopher's metaphysical arguments have had on his epistemological or ethical position. Are the positions he takes on various questions consistent with one another? Do his metaphysical presuppositions conflict with his epistemological claims? In the course of such an inquiry it may be useful to classify a philosopher as, for example, a materialist or an idealist, a rationalist or an empiricist. Such classification is no end in itself, of course, but it may provide insight into the influence that previous philosophers have had on a writer and into his influence on subsequent writers. It must be kept in mind that when we say that two philosophers are, for example, empiricists, we are saying that in some respects their positions are alike. But it is just as important to recognize the respects in which their positions differ.

Philosophers have never lived in a vacuum; their writings have always been influenced by the writings of other philosophers, as well as by the society in which they live. It is often useful to study one philosopher in the light of some preceding philosophical writings of which he takes cognizance in his writings. In this way, one may come to have a clearer grasp of the problems to which the philosopher has addressed himself and may thus be better able to understand his writings. An historian of philosophy is often interested in the fact that problems of a particular kind predominate in the writings of a given period. For example, Greek philosophy before Socrates was primarily concerned to discover the fundamental stuff of which the universe was composed. But with the philosophy of Socrates came a notable change in focus from man's environment to man himself and his relations to other men. To a philosopher, the questions that have been asked in philosophy are often as interesting as the answers that have been given.

14. Conclusion

Three points about the divisions within the body of philosophy must be emphasized. First, the areas are not independent of one another; rarely is any study in philosophy irrelevant to any other study in philosophy. Arguments in one area may be presupposed by the discussion of a problem, or even its formulation, in another. If, e.g., in the philosophy of science, one is investigating different methods for the confirmation of theories, he must have in mind some criterion for the adequacy of evidence. He may even attack his problem by first attempting to discover the epistemological assumptions of various methods of confirmation.

Second, it must not be assumed that the areas of inquiry discussed in this chapter are the sole province of the professional philosopher. Practicing scientists, for example, often seek to formulate and answer some of the questions here identified as philosophical, and some of the most creative work in logic has been done by mathematicians. It is a common mistake, fostered in part by the division of research areas in the modern university, to suppose that philosophic concerns and problems are completely separate from the concerns of scientists, lawyers, artists, physicians, etc.

Third, the demarcation of areas in philosophy is neither an exhaustive nor an unchanging classification. It is often neither possible nor important to decide to what area of inquiry a particular question belongs. Is the question of the tenability of the analytic–synthetic distinction an epistemological question or one for the philosophy of language? This question is moot, but inquiry into the analytic–synthetic distinction in no way presupposes any answer to this question. Some questions in philosophy underlie several specific studies: The question of the logical structure of explanations is as relevant to the philosophy of science as it is to the philosophy of history. And specific studies of historical and scientific explanations in turn shed light on the more general question of the nature of explanation.

This chapter will have served the purpose for which it was intended if the reader has gained from it some insight into the general problems to which philosophers have addressed themselves and is thereby better able to understand his readings in philosophy.

Bibliography

The following is a list of books and series that are of major importance in the development of analytic philosophy or are particularly helpful to the introductory student. All are by contemporary British and American authors. No attempt has been made to provide an exhaustive bibliography of contemporary analytic philosophy, nor are any books included that were written prior to the twentieth century or outside the current Anglo–American philosophical tradition.

The branches of philosophy to which each work listed is primarily relevant are indicated by capital letters following each entry according to the following code: A—anthology; B—series; C—philosophy of language; D—metaphysics; E —epistemology; F—philosophy of science; G—ethics and theory of value; H—aesthetics; I—philosophy of law; J— philosophy of religion; K—philosophy of history; L—logic and philosophy of logic; M—philosophy of mind; N—history of philosophy.

1. Ammerman, Robert R. (ed.). *Classics of Analytic Philosophy.* New York: McGraw-Hill, 1965. (A)
2. Anscombe, G. E. M. *Intention.* 2nd ed. Oxford: Basil Blackwell, 1963. (E, G, M)

3. ———, and P. T. Geach. *Three Philosophers*. Oxford: Basil Blackwell, 1961. (D, L, N)

4. Armstrong, D. M. *Perception and the Physical World*. New York: The Humanities Press, 1961. (See number 8.) (E, M)

5. Austin, J. L. *How to Do Things with Words*. Cambridge, Mass.: Harvard University Press, 1962. (C)

6. ———. *Philosophical Papers*. Oxford: The Clarendon Press, 1961. (C)

7. ———. *Sense and Sensibilia*. Oxford: The Clarendon Press, 1962. (E)
Paperback: New York: Oxford University Press, 1964 (Galaxy Books).

8. Ayer, A. J. (ed.). INTERNATIONAL LIBRARY OF PHILOSOPHY AND SCIENTIFIC METHOD. London: Routledge and Kegan Paul; New York: The Humanities Press. (B)

9. ———. *Language, Truth and Logic*. 2nd ed. London: V. Gollancz, 1946. (C, D, E, G, L)
Paperback: New York: Dover, 1952.

10. ———. *The Problem of Knowledge*. New York: St. Martin's Press, 1956. (E, M)
Paperback: Baltimore, Md.: Penguin Books, 1962.

11. Beardsley, Elizabeth, and Monroe Beardsley (eds.). THE PRENTICE-HALL FOUNDATIONS OF PHILOSOPHY SERIES (paperback series). Englewood Cliffs, N.J.: Prentice-Hall.
Aldrich, Virgil. *Philosophy of Art*.
Alston, William. *Philosophy of Language*.
Barker, Stephen. *Philosophy of Mathematics*.
Chisholm, Roderick. *Theory of Knowledge*.
Dray, William. *Philosophy of History*.
Frankena, William. *Ethics*.
Hempel, Carl. *Philosophy of Natural Science*.
Hick, John. *Philosophy of Religion*.
Hook, Sidney. *Political Philosophy*.
Lenz, John. *Philosophy of Education*.
Rudner, Richard. *Philosophy of Social Science*.
Salmon, Wesley. *Logic*.
Taylor, Richard. *Metaphysics*.

12. Berofsky, Bernard (ed.). *Free Will and Determinism*. New York: Harper & Row, 1966. (A, M, E)

13. Bird, Graham. *Kant's Theory of Knowledge*. New York: The Humanities Press, 1962. (See number 8.) (D, E, M, N)

14. Black, Max (ed.). CONTEMPORARY PHILOSOPHY. Ithaca, N.Y.: Cornell University Press. (B)

15. ———. *Problems of Analysis*. Ithaca, N.Y.: Cornell University Press, 1954. (A)

16. Braybrooke, David (ed.). *Philosophical Problems of the Social Sciences*. London: Macmillan, 1965. (F, E)

17. Broad, C. D. *Five Types of Ethical Theory*. London: Routledge and Kegan Paul, 1930. (See number 80.) (G, N)
18. Butler, R. J. (ed.). *Analytical Philosophy*. New York: Barnes & Noble, 1963. (A)
19. Carnap, Rudolf. *Introduction to Semantics, Studies in Semantics*, Vol. I. Cambridge, Mass.: Harvard University Press, 1942. (C, L)
20. ———. *Logical Syntax of Language*. London: Routledge and Kegan Paul, 1937. (C, L)
21. ———. *Meaning and Necessity*. Chicago: The University of Chicago Press, 1942. (C, L)
22. ———. *Philosophical Foundations of Physics*. Martin Gardner (ed.). New York: Basic Books, 1966. (E, F)
23. Casteneda, H.-N., and G. Nakhnikian (eds.). *Morality and the Language of Conduct*. Detroit, Mich.: Wayne State University Press, 1963. (A, G)
24. Caton, Charles Edwin (ed.). *Philosophy and Ordinary Language*. Urbana: University of Illinois Press, 1963 (paperback). (A, C)
25. Chappell, V. C. (ed.). *Ordinary Language*. Englewood Cliffs, N.J.: Prentice-Hall, 1964. (See number 35.) (A, C)
26. ———. *The Philosophy of Mind*. Englewood Cliffs, N.J.: Prentice-Hall, 1962 (paperback). (A, M)
27. Chisholm, Roderick M. *Perceiving*. Ithaca, N.Y.: Cornell University Press, 1957. (See number 14.) (E, G)
28. Chomsky, Noam. *Cartesian Linguistics: A Chapter in the History of Rationalist Thought*. New York: Harper & Row, 1966. (C, E, N)
29. Danto, Arthur, and Sidney Morgenbesser (eds.). *Philosophy of Science*. New York: Meridian Books, 1960 (paperback). (A, F)
30. Dray, William. *Laws and Explanation in History*. London: Oxford University Press, 1957. (F, K)
31. Elton, William (ed.). *Aesthetics and Language*. Oxford: Basil Blackwell, 1954. (A, H)
32. Feigl, Herbert, *et al.* (eds.). *Minnesota Studies in the Philosophy of Science*. Minneapolis: University of Minnesota Press. (A, B, F)
33. ———, and Wilfrid Sellars (eds.). *Readings in Philosophical Analysis*. New York: Appleton-Century-Crofts, 1949. (A)
34. ———, and May Brodbeck (eds.). *Readings in the Philosophy of Science*. New York: Appleton-Century-Crofts, 1953. (A, F)
35. Feinberg, Joel, and Wesley C. Salmon (eds.). CONTEMPORARY PERSPECTIVES IN PHILOSOPHY (paperback series). Englewood Cliffs, N.J.: Prentice-Hall. (B)
36. Flew, Antony G. N. (ed.). *Essays in Conceptual Analysis*. London: Macmillan, 1956. (A, C, D, E, F, L)
37. ——— (ed.). *Logic and Language* (First series). Oxford: Basil Blackwell, 1952. (A)

38. ———— (ed.). *Logic and Language* (Second series). Oxford: Basil Blackwell, 1953. (A)

39. ————. *Hume's Philosophy of Belief.* New York: The Humanities Press, 1961. (See number 8.) (D, E, J, M, N)

40. ————, and Alasdair MacIntyre (eds.). *New Essays in Philosophical Theology.* London: SCM Press, 1955. (A, D, J)

41. Fodor, Jerry, and Jerrold Katz (eds.). *Philosophy of Language.* Englewood Cliffs, N.J.: Prentice-Hall, 1964. (A, C)

42. ———— (eds.). *The Structure of Language.* Englewood Cliffs, N.J.: Prentice-Hall, 1964. (A, C, L)

43. Gardiner, Patrick (ed.). *Theories of History.* Glencoe, Ill.: The Free Press, 1959. (A, K)

44. Gombrich, E. H. *Art and Illusion.* New York: Bollingen Foundation, distributed by Pantheon Books, 1960. (H, E)

45. Goodman, Nelson. *Fact, Fiction and Forecast.* Cambridge, Mass.: Harvard University Press, 1955. (D, E, F)

46. Hampshire, Stuart. *Freedom and the Individual.* New York: Harper & Row, 1965. (D, E, G, M)

47. ————. *Thought and Action.* London: Chatto & Windus, 1959. (D, E, M)

48. Hare, R. M. *Freedom and Reason.* Oxford: The Clarendon Press, 1963. (G)

49. ————. *The Language of Morals.* Oxford: The Clarendon Press, 1952. (G)
Paperback: New York: Oxford University Press, 1964 (Galaxy Books).

50. Hart, H. L. A. *The Concept of Law.* Oxford: The Clarendon Press, 1961. (I)

51. ————, and A. M. Honore. *Causation in the Law.* Oxford: The Clarendon Press, 1959. (D, F, I)

52. Hempel, Carl G. *Fundamentals of Concept Formation in Empirical Science.* Chicago: The University of Chicago Press, 1952. (See number 79.) (F)

53. Holland, R. F. (ed.). STUDIES IN PHILOSOPHICAL PSYCHOLOGY. London: Routledge and Kegan Paul; New York: The Humanities Press. (B)

54. Hospers, John. *An Introduction to Philosophical Analysis.* Englewood Cliffs, N.J.: Prentice-Hall, 1963. (E, G)

55. Jeffrey, Richard C. *The Logic of Decision.* McGraw-Hill Series in Probability and Statistics. New York: McGraw-Hill, 1965. (E, L, H, G)

56. Kalish, Donald, and Richard Montague. *Logic: Techniques of Formal Reasoning.* New York: Harcourt, Brace & World, 1964. (L)

57. Katz, Jerrold J. *The Philosophy of Language.* New York: Harper & Row, 1966. (C)

58. Katz, Joseph, *et al.* (eds.). *Writers on Ethics.* Princeton, N.J.: Van Nostrand, 1962. (A, G)

59. Kaufmann, Walter Arnold. *Critique of Religion and Philosophy*. New York: Harper & Row, 1958. (G, J)

60. Kenny, Anthony. *Action, Emotion and Will*. London: Routledge and Kegan Paul, 1963. (See number 53.) (E, G, M)

61. Kuhn, Thomas S. *The Structure of Scientific Revolutions*. Chicago: The University of Chicago Press, 1962. (See number 79.) (F)

62. Kyburg, Henry E., Jr., and Howard E. Smokler (eds.). *Studies in Subjective Probability*. New York: John Wiley, 1964 (paperback). (A, F)

63. Lazerowitz, Morris. *The Structure of Metaphysics*. London: Routledge and Kegan Paul, 1953. (See number 80.) (D, E)

64. Lewis, C. I. *Mind and the World Order*. New York: Scribner, 1929. (D, E) Paperback: New York: Dover, 1956.

65. Linsky, Leonard. *Semantics and the Philosophy of Language*. Urbana: University of Illinois Press, 1952. (A, C)

66. MacDonald, Margaret (ed.). *Philosophy and Analysis*. Oxford: Basil Blackwell, 1954. (A)

67. Madden, Edward H. *The Structure of Scientific Thought*. Boston: Houghton Mifflin, 1960. (F)

68. Margolis, Joseph (ed.). *Philosophy Looks at the Arts*. New York: Scribner, 1964 (paperback). (A, H)

69. Mates, Benson. *Elementary Logic*. New York: Oxford University Press, 1965. (L, C)

70. Melden, A. I. (ed.). *Essays in Moral Philosophy*. Seattle: University of Washington Press, 1958. (A, G)

71. ———— (ed.). *Ethical Theories*. 2nd ed. Englewood Cliffs, N.J.: Prentice-Hall, 1961. (A, G)

72. Moore, G. E. *Principia Ethica*. Cambridge: Cambridge University Press, 1903. (G) Paperback: Cambridge: Cambridge University Press, 1962.

73. Morgenbesser, Sidney, and James Walsh (eds.). *Free Will*. Englewood Cliffs, N.J.: Prentice-Hall, 1962 (paperback). (A, G, M)

74. Morris, Herbert (ed.). *Freedom and Responsibility*. Stanford, Calif.: Stanford University Press, 1961. (A, G, I)

75. Nagel, Ernest. *Principles of the Theory of Probability*. Chicago: The University of Chicago Press, 1939. (See number 79.) (F)

76. ————. *The Structure of Science*. New York: Harcourt, Brace & World, 1961. (F)

77. ————, and Richard B. Brandt (eds.). *Meaning and Knowledge*. New York: Harcourt, Brace & World, 1965. (A, E, C, D)

78. Nakhnikian, George. *An Introduction to Philosophy*. New York: Knopf, 1967. (C, E, F, G)

79. Neurath, Otto, Rudolf Carnap, and Charles Morris (eds.). INTERNATIONAL ENCYCLOPEDIA OF UNIFIED SCIENCE. Chicago: The University of Chicago Press. (B)

80. Ogden, C. K. (ed.). INTERNATIONAL LIBRARY OF PHILOSOPHY, PSYCHOLOGY, AND SCIENTIFIC METHOD. London: Routledge and Kegan Paul. (B)
81. Pap, Arthur. *Elements of Analytic Philosophy.* New York: Macmillan, 1949.
82. ———. *An Introduction to the Philosophy of Science.* New York: The Free Press, 1962. (E, F)
83. Passmore, John A. *A Hundred Years of Philosophy.* London: G. Duckworth, 1957. (N)
84. Pears, D. F. (ed.). *Freedom and the Will.* New York: St. Martin's Press, 1963. (A, D, G, I, M)
85. Pitcher, George (ed.). *Truth.* Englewood Cliffs, N.J.: Prentice-Hall, 1964. (See number 35.) (A, C, L)
86. Quine, Willard Van Orman. *From a Logical Point of View.* 2nd ed. rev. Cambridge, Mass.: Harvard University Press, 1961. (C, D, L)
    Paperback: New York: Harper Torchbooks, 1963.
87. ———. *Methods of Logic.* 2nd ed. rev. New York: Henry Holt, 1959. (L)
88. ———. *Word and Object.* New York: John Wiley, 1960. (C, D, E, L, M)
89. Rader, Melvin. *A Modern Book of Esthetics.* 3rd ed. rev. New York: Holt, Rinehart and Winston, 1960. (A, H)
90. Reichenbach, Hans. *Elements of Symbolic Logic.* New York: The Free Press, 1966. (C, L)
91. Rorty, Richard (ed.). *The Linguistic Turn: Recent Essays in Philosophical Method.* Chicago: The University of Chicago Press, 1967. (A)
92. Russell, Bertrand. *Introduction to Mathematical Philosophy.* London: George Allen & Unwin, 1919. (L)
93. ———. *The Problems of Philosophy.* New York: Henry Holt, 1912. (D, E)
    Paperback: New York: Oxford University Press, 1959 (Galaxy Books).
94. Ryle, Gilbert. *The Concept of Mind.* London: Hutchinson's University Library, 1949. (E, M)
    Paperback: New York: Barnes & Noble, 1962.
95. ———. *Dilemmas.* Cambridge: Cambridge University Press, 1954. (C, D, M)
    Paperback: Cambridge: Cambridge University Press, 1959.
96. Scheffler, Israel. *The Anatomy of Inquiry.* New York: Knopf, 1963. (E, F)
97. Schilpp, Paul Arthur (ed.). THE LIBRARY OF LIVING PHILOSOPHERS. La Salle, Ill.: Open Court; London: Cambridge University Press. (B)
98. Scriven, Michael. *Primary Philosophy.* New York: McGraw-Hill, 1966. (C, E, F, G, H)

99. Sellars, Wilfrid, and John Hospers (eds.). *Readings in Ethical Theory*. New York: Appleton-Century-Crofts, 1952. (A, G)

100. Shapere, Dudley (ed.). *Philosophical Problems of Natural Science*. London: Macmillan, 1965. (F, E)

101. Sidgwick, Henry. *Outlines of the History of Ethics*. 6th ed. London: Macmillan, 1954. (G, N)
Paperback: Boston: Beacon Paperbacks, 1962.

102. Singer, Marcus George. *Generalization in Ethics*. New York: Knopf, 1961. (G)

103. Skyrms, Brian. *Choice and Chance: An Introduction to Inductive Logic*. Belmont, Calif.: Dickenson Press, 1966. (L, F, E)

104. Stevenson, Charles L. *Ethics and Language*. New Haven, Conn.: Yale University Press, 1944. (C, G)
Paperback: New Haven, Conn.: Yale University Press, 1960.

105. Strawson, P. F. *Individuals: An Essay in Descriptive Metaphysics*. London: Methuen, 1959. (C, D, L, M)
Paperback: Garden City, N.Y.: Anchor Books, 1963.

106. Suppes, Patrick. *Introduction to Logic*. Princeton, N.J.: Van Nostrand, 1957. (L)

107. Szasz, Thomas S., M.D. *Law, Liberty and Psychiatry*. New York: Macmillan, 1963. (E, F, G, I, M)

108. Toulmin, Stephen. *An Examination of the Place of Reason in Ethics*. Cambridge: Cambridge University Press, 1953. (F, G, J)
Paperback: Cambridge: Cambridge University Press, 1961.

109. Urmson, J. O. *Philosophical Analysis*. Oxford: The Clarendon Press, 1958. (C, D, E, L, N)

110. Vivas, Eliseo, and Murray Krieger (eds.). *The Problems of Aesthetics*. New York: Rinehart, 1953. (A, H)

111. Warnock, G. J. *Berkeley*. Baltimore, Md.: Penguin Books, 1953 (paperback). (C, E, J, M, N)

112. Warnock, Mary. *Ethics Since 1900*. London: Oxford University Press, 1960. (G, N)

113. Wasserstrom, Richard Alan. *The Judicial Decision*. Stanford, Calif.: Stanford University Press, 1961. (I)

114. Weitz, Morris (ed.). *20th-Century Philosophy: The Analytic Tradition*. Readings in the History of Philosophy Series, Paul Edwards and Richard H. Popkin (eds.). New York: The Free Press, 1966. (A)

115. Wilder, Raymond L. *Introduction to the Foundations of Mathematics*. New York: John Wiley, 1952. (L)

116. Wisdom, John. *Philosophy and Psycho-analysis*. Oxford: Basil Blackwell, 1953. (D, E, M)

117. Wittgenstein, Ludwig. *The Blue and Brown Books*. New York: Harper & Row, 1958. (C, E, M)

118. ———. *Lectures and Conversations on Aesthetics, Psychology and Religious Belief*. Cyril Barrett (ed.). Berkeley: University of California Press, 1966. (C, E, H, J, M)

119. ———. *Philosophical Investigations.* 3rd ed., G. E. M. Anscombe (tr.). New York: Macmillan, 1968 (C, D, E, F, G, H, L, M)
120. Wright, Georg Henrik von. *The Varieties of Goodness.* New York: The Humanities Press, 1963. (See number 8.) (G, M)

Index

'Deficiency', 121
Definiendum, 104
Definiens, 104
Definition, 101 ff.
Denotation, 78
Descartes, 99
Difference, 120
Disjunction, 13

'Efficiency', 121
Empiricism, 98, 156
Entailment, 45
'Entity', 121
Epistemology, 97 ff., 131 ff.,
    145
Ethics, 126 ff., 131, 152 ff.;
    see also Goodness
Evidence, 89 ff., 127 ff.,
    131 ff., 137, 150
Existence, 137
Existential quantifier, 31
Explanation, 141 ff., 148 ff.
Explication, 105 ff.
Extension, 78 ff.
Extensional Equivalence, 78
Extensional Sentences, 78 ff.

Frege, Gottlob, 80*n*

Goodness, 49 ff., 126 ff.

History, philosophy of, 148 ff.;
    of philosophy, 154 ff.

Hobbes, Thomas, 152
Hume, David, 99

Implication, 16 ff., 43
Incomplete Arguments, 8,
    103
Inconsistent Set, 21
Individual Variables, 30 ff.
Induction, 133
Inductive Arguments, 8, 103
Inference, 133
Instantiation, 66 ff.
Intension, 78 ff.
Intensional Equivalence, 79
Intensional Sentences, 79 ff.,
    146 ff.
Intersection of Sets, 40
Intuitive Accord, 105
'Is', 48

Jointly Exhaustive Properties,
    50 ff.

Kant, Immanuel, 89, 96, 99
Knowledge, 131 ff.

Language, philosophy of,
    144 ff.; *see also* Sen-
    tences; Meaning; Seman-
    tics; Intension
Law, philosophy of, 152 ff.

To:

....

From:

....

Date:

....

Here's a quick and fun way to share God's Word with those we love the most. The *Stop-and-Go Devotional* is a must-have resource for every busy parent!

—**Brian Jones**, senior pastor and author of *Finding Favor: God's Blessings Beyond Health, Wealth, and Happiness*

If you're a busy parent looking for fast but meaningful family devotions, the book you hold might just be for you—with best-loved Bible stories, talking points, prayers, and activities even the busiest family will be able to use. Pause, ponder, pray, and practice sharing God's love with the *Stop-and-Go Devotional*!

—**Glenys Nellist**, author of *Love Letters from God* and the Snuggle Time series

These adorable devotions are just the right size for young children, with action worked into each one—from singing to marching to packing a suitcase! A perfect way to work out the wiggles while you wiggle some wisdom into young hearts.

—**Bonnie Rose Hudson**, author at WriteBonnieRose.com and director of SchoolhouseTeachers.com

Stop-and-Go Devotional will have your kids begging for devotional time every day. The quick daily reads build a foundation of God's Word in your child while instilling a love for Bible time. Noise-making words sprinkled throughout the engaging stories make this extra fun to read aloud and is sure to keep the listener's attention. Thoughtful, age-appropriate questions, simple prayers, and action steps that get them up and moving will surely have your kids asking for you to read just one more!

—**Angela Mills**, preschool teacher and author of *Bless Your Husband: Creative Ways to Encourage and Love Your Man*

STOP-AND-GO
DEVOTIONAL

STOP

GO

52 DEVOTIONS FOR BUSY FAMILIES

DIANE STORTZ
ILLUSTRATED BY HANNAH MARKS

An Imprint of Thomas Nelson

Stop-and-Go Devotional

© 2019 by Diane Stortz

Published in Nashville, Tennessee, by Tommy Nelson. Tommy Nelson is an imprint of Thomas Nelson. Thomas Nelson is a registered trademark of HarperCollins Christian Publishing, Inc.

Published in association with the Books & Such Literary Management, 52 Mission Circle, Suite 122, PMB 170, Santa Rosa, California 95409, www.booksandsuch.com.

Illustrated by Hannah Marks.

Tommy Nelson titles may be purchased in bulk for educational, business, fund-raising, or sales promotional use. For information, please e-mail SpecialMarkets@ThomasNelson.com.

Scripture quotations marked ESV are taken from the ESV® Bible (The Holy Bible, English Standard Version®). Copyright © 2001 by Crossway, a publishing ministry of Good News Publishers. Used by permission. All rights reserved.

Scripture quotations marked GNT are taken from the Good News Translation in Today's English Version—Second Edition. Copyright 1992 by American Bible Society. Used by permission.

Scripture quotations marked ICB are taken from the International Children's Bible®. Copyright © 1986, 1988, 1999, 2015 by Thomas Nelson. Used by permission. All rights reserved.

Scripture quotations marked KJV are taken from the King James Version. Public domain.

Scripture quotations marked NIV are taken from the Holy Bible, New International Version®, NIV®. Copyright © 1973, 1978, 1984, 2011 by Biblica, Inc.® Used by permission of Zondervan. All rights reserved worldwide. www.zondervan.com. The "NIV" and "New International Version" are trademarks registered in the United States Patent and Trademark Office by Biblica, Inc.®

Scripture quotations marked NLT are taken from the Holy Bible, New Living Translation. © 1996, 2004, 2007, 2013 by Tyndale House Foundation. Used by permission of Tyndale House Publishers, Inc., Carol Stream, Illinois 60188. All rights reserved.

ISBN-13: 978-1-4003-1758-5

Library of Congress Cataloging-in-Publication Data is on file.

Printed in China

19 20 21 22 23 DSC 6 5 4 3 2 1

Mfr: DSC / Shenzhen, China / February 2019 / PO #9520577

For Roman, always on the go

CONTENTS

NEW TESTAMENT STORIES

LETTER TO PARENTS

Dear Busy Parents,

The stories in this book show God's strong love, goodness, and power. What better stories for energetic preschoolers and primary-grade children than accounts from the Bible filled with action, adventure, and the assurance that God always loves us?

And what better way to engage young children with these stories than with devotions crafted especially for them and your busy family?

Each devotion provides

- a short, action-filled story to **Stop and Read**,
- talking points, questions, and a prayer you can use to **Think and Talk**, plus
- an activity to do together, a thought to remember, and a supporting Bible verse—**Green Means Go!**

You can do one devotion each day or spread out the material over a year by doing one each week—whatever works best for your family.

I'm praying this book helps you take advantage of ordinary moments in the day when you and your child can **STOP** for a moment to hear God's truths, SLOW to think about them together, and then GO into the world with His love in your hearts!

Diane Stortz

OLD
TESTAMENT
STORIES

SEVEN SUPER DAYS

GENESIS 1–2

In the beginning, out of nothing, God made everything.

Day 1: God said, "Light!" The dark ran away. God called the light *day*, and He called the dark *night*.

Day 2: God said, "Sky!" Blue sky sparkled way up high.

Day 3: "Dry ground!" God said. The land rose up with seas all around. "Plants, grass, and trees!" God said. **Pop! Pop! Pop!** Plants, grass, and trees burst out of the ground!

God's wonderful story had begun.

Day 4: God said, "Sun, moon, and stars!"

Day 5: God said, "Fish to **splash!** Birds that **zoom!**"

Day 6: "Animals of all kinds!" Everything God made was good.

Next came the best part. "People!" God said. "They will care for the earth and work the land." God made a man named Adam and a woman named Eve.

"Yes," God said. "It's very good!"

Day 7: God rested.

THINK AND TALK

God's beautiful world shows us how wonderful He is! From the tiniest bug to the tallest giraffe, from the deepest ocean to the highest mountain, God thought of it all, and He made it all. No one else could ever do that! God is our Creator. He made the first people, and He made you!

- What do you like to play when you're outside in God's wonderful world?

- What is something God made that you really like to see?

> Dear God, Your beautiful world helps me know You are wonderful! Thank You for making the world—and me! Amen.

Find your crayons or markers. Get these colors: red, blue, green, yellow, and purple. In your yard or at the park, match the colors of your crayons or markers to the colors in God's beautiful world.

• • • ● ● ● • • •

REMEMBER
God made the world.

"I am the LORD, who made all things."

—ISAIAH 44:24 NLT

DELICIOUS?

GENESIS 3

Adam and Eve lived in a garden. A slithery snake inched his way to the middle of the garden and asked Eve, "Feeling hungry? Try some fruit from the Tree of Knowing Good and Evil."

"God told us not to," said Eve.

"The fruit won't hurt you," lied the snake. "You'll be wise like God, that's all."

The fruit looked delicious, and Eve wanted to be as wise as God. She picked some fruit and ate it. **Crunch. Munch.** She handed some to Adam, and he ate it too. *Mmm. Yum.*

But something felt terribly wrong. Something *was* terribly wrong! Adam and Eve had made a big mistake.

God told the snake, "From now on, you will crawl on your belly."

Then God told Adam and Eve, "You will have pain in your lives from now on. You will have to work hard for your food. And you cannot live forever anymore." So God put Adam and Eve out of the garden and sent strong angels to guard the way back in.

But someday, God promised, Someone would come to make things right again!

THINK AND TALK

God, our Creator, tells us what is best for us because He loves us so much. When Adam and Eve didn't do what God said, they didn't get a good result. We can always believe that what God says is good for us, and we should always listen and obey.

- Why does God tell us what is best for us?

- Whom do you think God planned to send to make things right again? (Jesus!)

Dear God, You know what is best. I want to listen to You and do what You say. Amen.

With some friends and a grown-up, play Simon Says. Choose one person to be Simon. Simon gives commands that start with "Simon says," such as "Simon says rub your tummy" or "Simon says hop on one foot." But sometimes Simon does not say "Simon says" when he or she gives a command.

If a command begins with "Simon says," obey the command or you'll be out. But if the command does *not* begin with "Simon says," *don't* do it or you'll be out. Listen closely and follow the right commands!

• • ● ● ● ● ● • •

REMEMBER
God knows what is best.

Follow all his ways.

—1 KINGS 2:3 NLT

AFLOAT ON A BOAT

GENESIS 6–7

Noah," said God, "I'm sending a flood. Build a big boat. I'll keep you safe."

Noah believed God, so he got busy.

Zoomfa. Zoomfa. Noah and his sons cut wood.

They hammered the pieces together to form the boat. **Rat-a-tat-tat!**

They coated the boat with tar so it would float, and Mrs. Noah gathered food to take on board.

People laughed at Noah while he worked. "Ha-ha! Tee-hee! Silly old Noah. What's he doing? How can the earth flood? We've never even seen rain."

Noah kept on building. And when the boat was done, two by two, animals of every kind came to the boat. They marched inside with Noah and his family, and God closed the door.

Slowly at first, then faster and harder, rain poured down for forty days and forty nights. **Pitter-patter, tap-tap-tap!** But Noah's big boat floated on the water, and everyone inside stayed safe and dry.

THINK AND TALK

God said He would keep Noah, his family, and the animals safe when the flood came, and He did. God keeps His promises! Just like Noah, we can believe what God says because His words are always true.

- What does it mean to keep a promise?

- What special book can we read to hear God's words to us?

> Dear God, Your plans are good and Your words are true! Help me listen to You and do what You say. Amen.

Sing these words about Noah's big boat to the tune of "This Old Man":

Noah's boat, Noah's boat.
God kept Noah's boat afloat.
That's what He promised, and His words are always true.
I trust God, and so can you!

. . • • ● ● • • . .

REMEMBER
God keeps His promises.

Your words are true.

—2 Samuel 7:28 icb

ROAD TRIP!

GENESIS 12

Pack your bags," God told Abraham. "Go to a new land. I'll point the way. I'm going to bless you and make you famous. All the people of the earth will be blessed through you."

Abraham obeyed God.

"Round up the sheep and goats," he told his workers. "Pack some tents. Load up the camels and donkeys. We're moving out!"

Clang! Clatter! Abraham and his wife, Sarah, packed cooking pots and pitchers, blankets, clothes, and coins. They stuffed bags with grain and fruit. They filled water jugs for the journey.

Camels bellowed. Donkeys brayed. They were ready for a road trip too.

Abraham looked at all the packed-up things. He looked at all the animals and people. "Let's go!" he said. Abraham wasn't sure where he was going, but he trusted God to lead him. And God did!

God led Abraham to Canaan. "This is the land I will give to you and your family," God said.

THINK AND TALK

In a crowded place, your mom or dad probably says, "Stay close and follow me." Maybe you hold hands too, and Mom or Dad leads the way. Abraham didn't know where he was going, but he followed as God led him to the Promised Land. God took care of Abraham all the way. God takes care of us when we follow His plans, and God's plans are always good!

- How do you think Abraham felt when he got to the Promised Land?

- Have you ever taken a long trip? Where did you go?

> Dear God, thank You for Your good plans for Abraham and for me. Amen.

Find your backpack or ask a grown-up for a small suitcase. Pretend you are going with Abraham on his journey. Pack your backpack or suitcase for the trip. What will you take with you?

• • • • • • •

REMEMBER
God's plans are always good.

The LORD will work out his plans for my life.

—PSALM 138:8 NLT

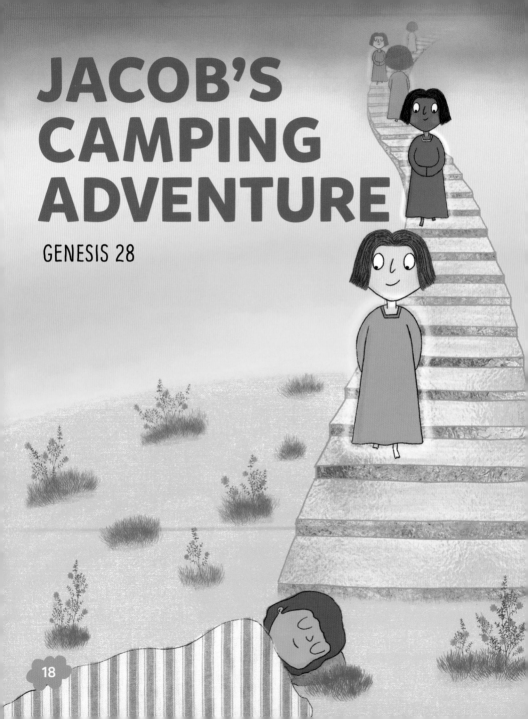

JACOB'S CAMPING ADVENTURE

GENESIS 28

Jacob, one of Abraham's grandsons, was grown up and ready to get married. He went on a journey to visit his relatives and find a wife.

"Good-bye!" Jacob called to his mother and father and started on his long walk through the countryside to his uncle's house.

"Here's a good place to camp," Jacob said as the sun went down. He yawned. He stretched. He found a rock for a pillow. He fell asleep and dreamed.

In his dream, Jacob saw a ladder so tall it reached from earth to heaven. Angels climbed up and down the ladder, and at the top stood God.

"Jacob," God said, "I promised this land to your grandfather Abraham and to your father, Isaac. My promise is for you too. Your family will be a blessing to everyone on earth. I will watch over you wherever you go, and I will bring you back to this land."

Jacob woke up. "God is here, and I didn't know it!" he said.

In the morning, Jacob picked up his rock pillow. Thwack! He stood it on one end. It would always remind him of his dream and God's promise.

Jacob might have been lonely or afraid as he walked many miles by himself, but he learned that God was with him the whole time! God is always with you too. He sees you and gives you just what you need because He loves you.

- Have you ever felt afraid or lonely? Where were you, and what did you do?

- How can you remember that God is always with you wherever you go?

> Dear God, thank You for loving me and going with me wherever I go. Thank You for taking care of me. Amen.

GREEN MEANS GO!

Camp out in the backyard or somewhere inside your house. What will you use for a pillow? When you go to sleep and when you wake up, remember that God is with you!

• • • • ● ● ● • • •

REMEMBER
God is always with you.

"The LORD your God is with you wherever you go."

—JOSHUA 1:9 ESV

DREAM TELLER

GENESIS 37; 39–46

One of Jacob's sons was Joseph. Joseph's brothers were mean to him and sold him as a slave. Joseph worked for a man named Potiphar in Egypt, far away.

At Potiphar's house, Joseph got in trouble for something he didn't do! Potiphar put Joseph into prison. The prison door locked with a loud **click!**

Two of the other prisoners were servants of the king. They had dreams they couldn't understand. With God's help, Joseph told them the meaning of their dreams. One servant said, "When I get out of here, I'll help you get out too." But he forgot his promise.

Later the king had a dream. Then the king's servant remembered Joseph. "Bring Joseph here now!" the king said.

With God's help, Joseph told the king the meaning of his dream. In seven years, no crops would grow! People would be hungry. "You must store up grain now," Joseph said.

"I will put you in charge!" the king answered.

During those years when no crops grew, Joseph's hungry brothers traveled to Egypt to buy grain.

"My brothers!" Joseph cried, and he hugged them. "You sold me as a slave, but God brought me here to save your lives!" So Joseph's brothers and his father, Jacob, moved to Egypt, where there was plenty of food.

Sometimes bad things happen to us, and we feel sad or angry or scared. But God is always with us. He'll take care of us like He took care of Joseph, and if we love and trust Him, He will bring something good out of the bad things.

- What is the best thing that has ever happened to you?

- What is something bad that has happened? What is something good that came from that?

> Dear God, thank You for the good things that happen, and thank You for making good out of the bad things too. Amen.

Joseph hugged his brothers when he saw them again. Give the people in your family a big hug today!

· • •●●●●• • ·

REMEMBER
God makes bad things turn out for good.

I will praise him for what he has done.

—Isaiah 63:7 ICB

A BABY, A BASKET, AND A BIG SISTER

EXODUS 1–2

As the years passed, Jacob's family became bigger and bigger. They were known as the Hebrews. A new king in Egypt thought his country had too many Hebrews. "Don't let your boy babies live," he told them. **Oh no!** One mother, named Jochebed, made a plan to keep her baby safe.

Jochebed hid the baby from the Egyptians until he was three months old, when he was too big (and too noisy) to hide any longer. Then she made him a basket boat. She painted a basket with tar to keep the water out. She put the baby in the basket and laid it gently among the tall grasses growing beside the Nile River.

Moses' big sister, Miriam, stood back and watched to see what would happen.

The princess of Egypt came to the river with her friends and found the baby in his basket, crying. **Waaah!** The princess felt sorry for him. "This must be one of the Hebrew children," she said.

Miriam ran to the princess. "Should I find one of the Hebrew women to nurse the baby for you?" she asked.

"Yes, please do," the princess said. So Miriam hurried home to get Jochebed—the baby's own mother!

Later on, the princess adopted the baby as her son and named the baby Moses. He grew up in the palace. Even though he was a Hebrew, he was safe.

God watched over baby Moses and kept him safe—in his basket boat, at home again with Jochebed, and in the palace as the princess's adopted son. God gives us families to love and help one another. Some children are born into their family, and some children are adopted into their family. Both kinds of families are part of God's wonderful plan!

➤ Who are the people in your family?

➤ What are some ways the people in your family love and help one another?

> Dear God, help me be a loving helper in my family. Thank You that families are part of Your plan! Amen.

Take a family photo and then print it out, or draw a picture of your family. Cut out a frame from construction paper or poster board and glue the frame over your picture. Write each person's name on the frame; then put your picture in a place where you'll see it every day. Thank God for each person in your family.

REMEMBER
God gives us families.

"Honor your father and your mother."

—Deuteronomy 5:16 ICB

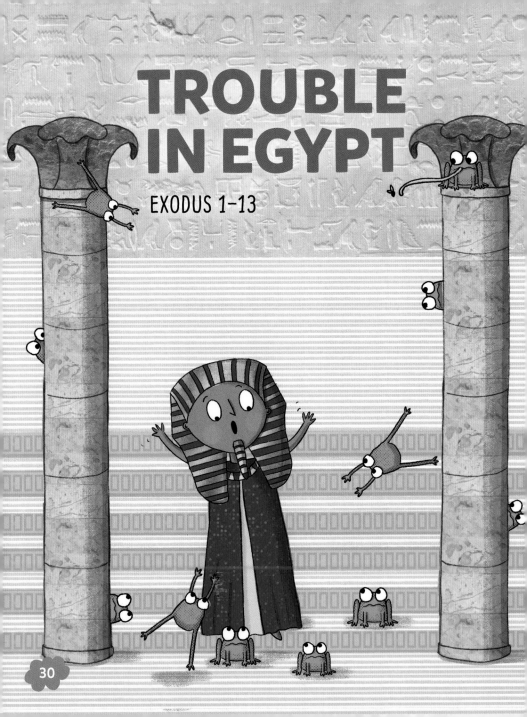

TROUBLE IN EGYPT

EXODUS 1–13

Jacob's big family became known as the Israelites. The new king of Egypt didn't like them.

"Too many Israelites!" said Pharaoh, the king. "They might try to take over. I will make them slaves." He made the Israelites work day and night.

"We need help!" the people cried, and God heard them. He called Moses, who was a grown-up now. "Moses!" God said. "Lead My people out of Egypt."

Moses went to see Pharaoh. "God wants His people to leave Egypt to worship Him," Moses said.

But Pharaoh said, "No! The people can't go!"

So God sent trouble to the land of Egypt.

First the river turned red, and no one could drink from it. Then frogs hopped everywhere, even inside houses. Gnats covered everyone like dust.

Then flies swarmed through the air—but not where the Israelites lived! Cattle got sick. People got painful sores on their skin. Hail hurt the crops, and grasshoppers ate what was left. But God kept the Israelites safe from all this trouble.

Whoosh! Darkness came over the lands of the Egyptians, but the Israelites had light. Some people died, but God protected His people.

Finally, Pharaoh said, "OK! You can go!"

The happy Israelites hurried out of Egypt.

THINK AND TALK

Pharaoh, the king, wanted the Israelites to stay in Egypt and work for him, but God wanted them to leave Egypt and go to a new land. What God wants is always best and right. God is King of the whole earth. We can listen to Him and do what He says!

- Count the troubles God sent to the land of Egypt. How many did you count?

- Who are the people you obey at home? At school? At church? Who is the King we *all* should obey?

> Dear God, You know what is best and right. You are King of the whole earth! Help me listen to You and obey. Amen.

GREEN MEANS GO!

In a dark room, put a blanket over chairs to make a tent. Turn on a big flashlight inside the tent. When God covered Egypt with darkness, He gave light to His people, the Israelites!

• • ●●●● • ••

REMEMBER
God is always right.

Tell the nations, "The Lord is king."

—PSALM 96:10 ICB

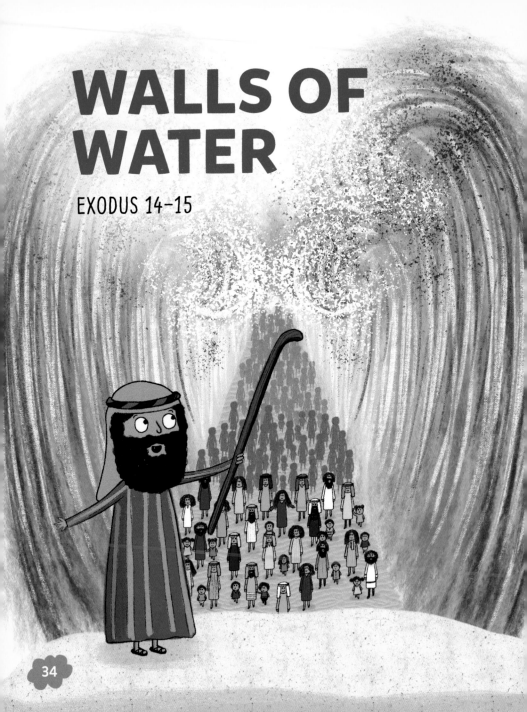

Pharaoh's army chased the Israelites after they left Egypt. The Israelites were trapped—the Red Sea was in front of them and the army was behind them! What could they do?

"Don't be afraid!" Moses said. "God will rescue you today. He will fight for you Himself. Stay calm and watch what happens."

A tall cloud moved between the Israelites and Pharaoh's army. The people kept walking toward the sea. God told Moses to hold his walking stick over the sea, and Moses obeyed.

WHOOSH! WHISH! God sent a strong wind. The wind blew a wide path through the sea. The people walked through the sea on dry ground between two walls of water!

Pharaoh's army rushed into the sea, chasing the Israelites. But God made their chariots hard to drive. "Let's get out of here!" shouted Pharaoh's soldiers.

When all the Israelites had crossed the sea, Moses raised his walking stick again. **Swish! Swoosh! SPLASH!** The walls of water crashed down.

Safe at last! The Israelites sang and danced, praising God.

The Israelites felt afraid when they were trapped between the Red Sea and Pharaoh's army. They didn't think God could help them. But just like God led His people out of Egypt, He led them through the sea. The Israelites could trust God to lead them, and we can trust Him to lead us too.

- Have you ever had a bad day? What happened? How did you feel?

- The next time you feel afraid or upset when something goes wrong, what will you do?

Dear God, You led the people through the Red Sea on dry ground! You always know the way! Please lead me every day, no matter what happens. Amen.

Play Follow the Leader with a friend or grown-up. Take turns being the leader. Whatever the leader does, everyone else does too. Make funny faces, walk like an elephant, do somersaults in the backyard—just follow the leader!

• • ● ● ● ● • •

REMEMBER
God leads us.

Lead me in the right path, O Lord.

—Psalm 5:8 NLT

TEN GOOD RULES

EXODUS 19–20

After God led His people out of Egypt, they camped in the wilderness on their way to the Promised Land. "I love My people," God said. "If they will obey Me, they will be My special treasure."

"We will obey!" the people told Moses.

"Get ready to worship!" Moses said. "God will meet with you in three days."

On the morning of the third day, thunder crashed and lightning flashed. The people heard a long, loud blast on a ram's horn. **Bwwahhh!** Everyone trembled.

Moses led the people out of the camp. They saw a mountain covered with smoke, and they knew God was there. The ram's horn blew again. **Bwwahhh!** The mountain shook.

Moses talked to God, and God answered in the thunder. God called Moses to the top of the mountain. The people watched Moses climb the mountain to meet with God.

"Here are the rules My people must obey," God said. He gave Moses ten good rules written on two large stones.

THINK AND TALK

Your family might have a "no candy before dinner" rule. Candy is a sweet treat, but it doesn't help you grow. If you fill up on candy before dinner, you won't be hungry for the good food your body needs to grow tall and strong. Just like your family has rules, God has rules for all His people. Rules keep us safe and tell us the right things to do.

- What are some of your family's rules? What are some rules for playing safely outside?

- Sometimes we don't want to follow the rules. What should we do then?

> Dear God, thank You for loving Your people and me! Thank You for Your ten good rules. Help me listen to You and do what You say. Amen.

With a grown-up, find Exodus 20:1–17 in the Bible and read God's ten good rules aloud. Then draw and decorate a big heart shape on a sheet of paper. Hang your heart where you will see it every day to remind you that God gives us good rules because He loves us.

• • • ● ● ● • • •

REMEMBER
God's rules are good for us.

I love your commands more than gold.

—PSALM 119:127 NLT

FUNNY FOOD

EXODUS 16

After they crossed the Red Sea and camped in the wilderness for a while, the Israelites began to miss their favorite foods. And they worried—how would they get enough food to eat out there in the desert?

They should have asked God for His help. They should have trusted God to feed them. But they didn't. Instead, they complained to Moses. **Grumble, grumble, grumble!**

"You're grumbling against God," Moses said, "not against me. Now here's what God will do. Every morning He will send you bread from heaven. Gather just enough to eat for one day."

The next morning the people looked outside. All around the camp was a thin layer of something white. It looked like frost. What was it?

It tasted sweet. **Yum!** They could make cereal or bake bread with it. The people called the funny food *manna*.

"Gather it up," Moses said. "Get just enough for today, because God will send more tomorrow. He will send what you need each day."

The people should have trusted God to send them manna every day, just as He said He would do. But some of them didn't. They gathered extra and saved it in their tents overnight. In the morning, the extra manna was full of worms. **Eew!**

God didn't let the Israelites go hungry. He provided manna for forty years.

THINK AND TALK

When we have a problem and don't know what to do, God knows what we need. He wants us to ask Him for His help; that's one way we show we trust Him. Another way we show we trust Him is by obeying Him—doing what He says. (Nobody wants to eat manna with worms in it!) We can always trust God to care for us.

- When is a time you asked God to help you? What did He do?

- When is a time that you obeyed God?

> Dear God, thank You that I can always trust You. Help me learn to trust You with everything and to do what You say. Amen.

With your family, start a list called "Ways We Trust God." Use words or pictures to make your list. Post the list and add to it every day this week.

• • ◦ ● ● ◉ ● ◦ • •

REMEMBER
God wants us to trust Him.

Trust in the LORD with all your heart.

—PROVERBS 3:5 NLT

CAN DONKEYS TALK?

NUMBERS 22

Come and visit me," the king told Balaam. "I have a job for you." But God told Balaam not to go.

Balaam obeyed God . . . at first. But when the king asked for him again, Balaam changed his mind. He saddled up his donkey and started off to see the king.

God sent an angel to block the road. Only the donkey could see the angel. "**Hee-haw!**" brayed the donkey, and she ran into a field.

Next the angel stood at a narrow place on the path between two vineyard walls. The donkey tried to *squeeeeze* around the angel. Balaam's foot scraped against the wall—**OW!** Balaam still couldn't see the angel.

When the angel moved farther down the road, the donkey stopped and plopped down right in front of him.

Balaam still couldn't see the angel. He yelled at the donkey and even hit her with a stick. Then God let the donkey talk!

"Why are you hitting me?" asked the donkey. "Have I ever done anything to hurt you?"

"Well, no," Balaam said.

Then God let Balaam see the angel too. Balaam bowed. "I've been wrong," he said. "I will do what God wants me to do."

THINK AND TALK

Angels are God's messengers. God sends angels to help His people. Balaam needed a lot of help to obey God—an angel *and* a talking donkey! Balaam's donkey wanted to do the right thing. Obeying God is always the right thing to do because God loves us and knows what is best. And only God can make a donkey talk!

- Why do you think God wants us to obey Him?

- How do we know God loves us?

Dear God, when I don't know what to do, Your rules show me what is right. Thank You for loving us and giving us Your good rules. Amen.

Make a "Pin the Mouth on the Donkey" game. On a large sheet of paper, draw the side view of a donkey. Post the drawing on a wall. Cut out a mouth from another sheet of paper and attach tape to the mouth. Now close your eyes and try to stick the mouth on the donkey.

REMEMBER
God wants us to obey Him.

Obey the commands of the Lord your God.

—Deuteronomy 4:2 icb

RUMBLE, TUMBLE!

JOSHUA 5–6

Standing outside the Israelites' camp, Joshua could see Jericho, a city with tall stone walls. Joshua knew God wanted the Israelites to live in this land, but how would they get past those walls?

Joshua saw someone else standing nearby, holding a sword. Who was this? "Are you a friend or enemy?" Joshua asked. It was an angel!

"I'm in charge of the Lord's army," the angel said.

"I'm at your service!" Joshua said. "What should I do?"

This is what the angel said: "Get your fighting men and march around Jericho once a day for six days. Seven priests must blow their horns. On the seventh day, march around Jericho seven times. Then shout! The walls of Jericho will fall down."

Joshua rounded up the people. "Line up!" he said. "March with me around the city walls. Don't talk. The priests will blow their horns, and God will be with us."

The people obeyed. Left, right. Left, right. Every day for six days, they marched around the tall stone walls of Jericho.

On the seventh day, the people marched around the city seven times. Then Joshua yelled, "Shout!" and all the people shouted.

Rrrumble! Tumble! The strong walls of Jericho came crashing down!

What do you like to play outside? Do you like to run races, play soccer, go up the climbing wall, or jump on the trampoline? Our bodies need exercise, and using our muscles makes us grow strong and powerful. But only God has the power to do impossible things, like making walls fall down with just a shout!

- Joshua and his men obeyed God's instructions. But who made the walls fall down?

- Is anyone or anything more powerful than God?

> Dear God, thank You for Your strong power. Help me always listen to You and believe You will do what You say! Amen.

GREEN MEANS GO!

March around the room while you chant these words aloud.
Or you can sing the words to the tune of "Ring Around the
Rosy." Be sure and fall down at the end like the walls of
Jericho did!

March around the city,
Just the way God told us.
Rumble, tumble!
The walls fall down!

·•●●●●•··

REMEMBER
God can do anything.

He has shown his people his power.

—Psalm 111:6 ICB

KINDNESS COUNTS

RUTH 1–4

I'm leaving Moab and going home to Bethlehem," Naomi told Ruth, her daughter-in-law. "My husband and my sons have died. You stay here and go back to your mother's house."

"I want to go with you and help you," Ruth said. "Your God will be my God." Ruth and Naomi walked together on miles of dusty roads.

In Bethlehem, Ruth picked up grain in a field. She filled her basket with barley so Naomi could bake bread.

"Who is that young woman?" asked Boaz, the owner of the field.

"That's Ruth from the land of Moab," his workers said.

"Stay here in my field," Boaz told Ruth. "Gather all the grain you want. Drink water from our well."

"Thank you, sir," Ruth said. "I don't deserve such kindness."

"You came here to help Naomi," Boaz said. "You trusted God to care for you. May God reward you for what you have done."

Soon Boaz married Ruth! Then they had a baby boy. **Waaa! Waaa!** They named the baby Obed. Naomi was a happy grandma now!

Ruth treated Naomi with kindness, and Boaz noticed. God noticed too. God is kind to us. He gave Ruth and Naomi a new family to love, including a baby boy. What a sweet blessing!

- **When has someone been kind to you?**

- **What could you do to be kind to someone else?**

> Dear God, thank You for Your kindness to us. Help me be kind like Ruth every day. Amen.

With help from a grown-up, grind some barley (or oatmeal) into flour in a blender. Use the flour to bake biscuits or bread, just like Ruth and Naomi did.

• • ● ● ● ● • ••

REMEMBER
God is kind to us.

The LORD is . . . kind in all his works.

—PSALM 145:17 ESV

HOW DO YOU FEEL?

1 SAMUEL 1

Every year, Hannah and her husband traveled to the tabernacle to celebrate and worship God.

And this year, like every year, Hannah ended up crying. She longed to have a baby, but she had no children. Her husband's other wife always made fun of Hannah because she had children and Hannah did not.

So this time Hannah went off by herself to pray to God at the tabernacle. She told Him how much she wanted a child and how sad she felt. "If I could have a son," she prayed, "he would always serve You. **I promise.**"

Eli, the priest at the tabernacle, saw Hannah crying and praying. Her mouth was moving but no words were coming out because she was praying in her heart. Eli wondered what was going on.

"I've been praying because I am so troubled," Hannah said. "I've been telling God how sad I feel."

"Then go in peace," Eli said. "The Lord has heard your prayer."

Hannah felt much better now! And God did answer her prayer. Hannah had a baby boy. She named him Samuel.

THINK AND TALK

God cares about our emotions (how we feel). When we feel sad, He wants to help us. When we tell Him all about our problems and ask for His help, we feel better. He is always glad to listen to us, whatever we have to say.

- How many different emotions can you name?

- What is something that makes you feel sad? What could you tell God about that?

> Dear God, thank You for caring about my feelings and listening to me when I feel sad. I love you. Amen.

Cut out three or four egg shapes; then cut them in half horizontally (or use plastic Easter eggs). Draw happy, sad, and mad facial expressions on the eggs—eyes on the top halves and mouths on the lower halves. Talk about what to do when you feel each emotion. Then have fun mixing up the eyes and mouths to create some funny new expressions.

· · • ◦ ● ● ◦ • · ·

REMEMBER
God cares when we're sad.

You comfort me and make me glad.

—Psalm 94:19 GNT

WHO'S CALLING?

1 SAMUEL 3

Young Samuel helped Eli the priest at the big tent where people worshipped God. At night Samuel slept inside the tent to guard it.

One night when Samuel was sleeping, a voice called, "Samuel!"

Samuel jumped up from his bed. He ran to Eli. **Thump, thump, thump!** "Did you call me?" Samuel asked. "Here I am. What do you need?"

"I didn't call you," Eli said. "Go back to bed."

The voice called again, "Samuel!"

Thump, thump, thump! Samuel ran to Eli. "Here I am," he said. "Did you call me?"

"I didn't call you," Eli said. "Go back to bed."

"Samuel!"

Thump, thump, thump! Samuel ran to Eli. "Here I am," he said. "Did you call me?"

"It is God calling you," Eli said. "If you hear the voice again, say, 'Speak, Lord. Your servant is listening.'"

"Samuel!" God called again. Samuel sat up and said, "Speak, Lord. I'm listening."

God gave Samuel an important message. From then on, Samuel served God all his life.

THINK AND TALK

Even though Samuel was young, God had something to tell him, and Samuel listened to what God said. God has things to tell you too, even though you are young. We can listen to what God says by reading the Bible. The Bible is God's message to us. It tells us all about Him!

- When do you hear and listen to God's words from the Bible?

- What Bible verse have you learned by heart?

Dear God, thank You for loving us and wanting to talk with us. Thank You for the Bible, Your Word to us. Amen.

Play a listening game. Sit outside or inside with a grown-up or a friend. Close your eyes. What are all the different sounds you can hear?

• • • • • • • • •

REMEMBER
God speaks to us.

Listen to the words of the Lord your God.

—Joshua 3:9 ICB

INSIDE OUT

1 SAMUEL 16

Who would lead Israel after King Saul?
"Go to Bethlehem, to Jesse's house," God told the prophet Samuel. "I have chosen one of Jesse's sons to be the next king. Anoint him with oil as a sign that he is my choice. I will show you who it is when you are there."

Samuel went to Bethlehem and invited Jesse and his sons to dinner. When Samuel saw the oldest son, Eliab, who was tall and handsome, Samuel thought Eliab would be God's choice.

"No, he's not the one," God said. "People judge by how someone looks. I look at the heart."

Samuel met six more of Jesse's sons, **1-2-3-4-5-6**, but none of them was the one God had chosen. "Do you have any other sons?" Samuel asked.

"The youngest is in the fields, taking care of the sheep," Jesse said.

"Call him to come here," Samuel said.

When David arrived at Samuel's dinner, God told Samuel, "He is the one. Anoint him."

So Samuel poured a flask of oil over David's head as a sign that he would be the next king.

THINK AND TALK

God doesn't judge us by how we look on the outside. He cares about our hearts, what kind of people we are on the inside—how we think and how we act. Are we kind and loving to others? Do we love Him? That's what God says is most important.

- Do you care more about how someone looks or about how someone acts?

- How could you be a friend to someone who looks different from you?

Dear God, thank You for caring about who we are on the inside, not on the outside. Help me have a heart that pleases You. Amen.

With tape, wrap two bath tissue tubes together. Then tape a length of yarn or ribbon to both tubes at one end to hang your "binoculars" around your neck. Wear them at meals this week to remind you to look at how others think and act, not how they look.

· · ● ● ● ● ● · ·

REMEMBER
God looks at the heart.

Your instructions are written on my heart.

—Psalm 40:8 NLT

SHEPHERD'S SONG

1 SAMUEL 17; PSALM 23

David had been anointed as the next king, but for now he was still a shepherd. He led his sheep to fields where they could eat good green grass—**munch, munch, crunch!**—and where they could take a nap when they were full. He took them to quiet streams where they could drink good clean water. **Slurp!**

As David led his sheep from place to place, he made sure they stayed on the right path and didn't stray away. (But if a sheep did get lost, David searched until he found it.)

David kept his sheep safe from wild animals too, like hungry lions and bears who thought a sheep would make a fine dinner. David fought them off with his slingshot and a club.

While the sheep rested, David thought about God. Sometimes he played music on his lyre and sang songs to praise God. When he got older, David wrote songs called *psalms* that we can read in the Bible. One of his songs tells us how God is like a shepherd!

All his life—as a shepherd and as king—David loved God, and he loved praising God too!

We have so many *reasons* to praise God. For starters, He's our Creator and He's good to us! We have so many *times* to praise Him—in the morning when we get up, at mealtimes, at bedtime, and more! We have so many *ways* to praise God too! We can sing, we can talk about Him, and we can do kind deeds to show we love Him. God loves to see and hear our praise.

- **What are some things we can praise God for?**

- **Why do you think God wants us to praise Him?**

> Dear God, thank You for who You are and for all You do for me. I praise You today! Amen.

Choose a way to praise God. You could sing a song, paint a picture, do cartwheels, or make a list of reasons to love God. What other ways could you praise Him?

• • • ● ● ● • • •

REMEMBER
God sees and hears our praise.

Give praise to the Lord your God!

—1 Chronicles 29:20 NLT

A GIANT SURPRISE

1 SAMUEL 17

Every day the Philistine and the Israelite armies lined up for battle. In the Philistine army was a giant named Goliath.

Nine-foot-tall Goliath stomped his giant-size feet. He waved his giant-size spear. "I'm not afraid of the army of Israel!" he yelled. "Send someone over to fight me."

"The giant is making fun of God!" David said. "But don't worry about Goliath. I will fight him."

"Don't be silly," said the king. "He's a giant. You're a boy."

"I'm a shepherd," David said. "I save my sheep from lions and bears. God will help me fight this giant." David picked up five smooth stones from a stream. He put them in his shepherd's bag and marched toward the giant.

"Who do you think you are?" Goliath roared. "You can't hurt *me*!"

"I'm coming in the name of the Lord," David said. "Today everyone will see that God rescues His people but not with swords and spears!"

David put a stone in his sling and hurled it at Goliath. The stone hit Goliath in the head, and he fell down with a giant-size **THUD**.

God used David to rescue His people from their enemies!

David didn't like it when Goliath made fun of God. He wanted everyone to know about God's goodness and power. David wasn't afraid of Goliath because David knew God was with him and would take care of him.

- If you know people who make fun of God, how could you pray for them? What could you say to them?

- Has anyone ever made fun of you or bullied you? Be sure to tell a grown-up and ask for help. God wants you to be safe, and He will help you.

> Dear God, thank You for how You save and take care of Your people. Thank You for taking care of me. Amen.

Lie on the floor. Ask a grown-up to place books or blocks on the floor beside you from your heels to the top of your head. Measure the line. That's how tall you are. Then make another line of books or blocks nine feet long—that's how tall Goliath was!

· · ● ● ● ● · · ·

REMEMBER
God rescues His people.

Our God is a God who saves us.

—Psalm 68:20 ICB

BIRD FOOD

1 KINGS 16–17

God told His people to worship only Him. But King Ahab didn't obey.

God sent Elijah to King Ahab with a message: "There will be no dew or rain during the next few years until I give the word," Elijah said.

No rain meant no crops. No crops meant no food. So Elijah's message made King Ahab angry.

"Hide from the king," God told Elijah. "Stay by the Kerith Brook. Drink water from the brook. Eat what the ravens bring you. I have given them orders to bring food to you."

Elijah did what God said. He set up camp near the Kerith Brook. When he was thirsty, he drank from the brook. Every morning he watched for the ravens. They swooped into his campsite with pieces of bread and meat in their big beaks. Every evening Elijah watched for the ravens too, and every evening they came back with more bread and meat.

"**Caw! Caw!**" the ravens said. Bread and meat for Elijah to eat—just as God promised!

THINK AND TALK

Elijah was a prophet. He told God's people things God wanted them to know. Elijah obeyed God, and God took care of Elijah. He kept Elijah safe and gave him food. God takes care of you too! He gave you a family to help you stay safe and to give you good food to eat.

- Who cooks food for your family? What's your favorite food?

- What is a rule in your family that keeps you safe?

> Dear God, thank You for all the ways You keep me safe and give me what I need! I love You, God. Amen.

Have an "Elijah snack." Drink water, just like Elijah did. Ask a grown-up to cut a slice of bread into small pieces. Cut some cooked meat into small pieces too. Pretend you are Elijah, eating the food the ravens brought.

· • • ● ● ● • • ·

REMEMBER
God protects and provides.

You prepare a feast for me.

—Psalm 23:5 NLT

NAAMAN'S DECISION

2 KINGS 5

Naaman, the army commander of Aram, had a terrible skin disease. Who would help him?

"Naaman should go see Elisha, God's prophet in Israel," a young girl said.

So Naaman traveled to Israel with his horses, chariots, and army officers. He went to Elisha's house.

Elisha sent a message out to Naaman: "Go wash yourself in the Jordan River seven times. Then God will heal you."

"What?" Naaman said. "I'm a very important person! Elisha should have come out and healed me himself."

But Naaman's army officers said, "If you were told to do a hard thing, you would do it. This is an easy thing. So you should do it."

Naaman thought about that. He wanted to get well, so he decided to obey. He went to the Jordan River and bobbed in the water seven times. **Plop! Splish! Splash! Splat! Swish! Swash! Swish!** And on the seventh time, Naaman's skin looked smooth and new.

Naaman went back to see Elisha. "Now I know there is no other God in all the world except the Lord!" he said.

THINK AND TALK

When you get a scrape or a bit of a stomachache, it hurts for a while, but then you get better. God made our bodies able to heal most of the time! Sometimes we need medicine or a visit to the doctor or hospital; sometimes we have to wait awhile to be well, but God is taking care of us the whole time.

- **When is a time that you got hurt or sick? How did you get better?**

- **Do you think you would like to be a nurse or doctor someday? Why or why not?**

> Dear God, thank You for making my body so it can heal. Thank You for helping me get well and stay well. Amen.

Go outside and fill a dishpan with water. Find an old doll or toy to bob up and down in the water seven times, like Namaan did.

· • • ● ● ● • • ·

REMEMBER
God heals our bodies.

"I am the Lord who heals you."

—Exodus 15:26 ICB

LOST AND FOUND

2 CHRONICLES 34

"The temple where we worship God needs to be fixed,"
said good King Josiah. "Let's get to work!"

Zoomfa. Zoomfa. Bam, bam, tap! Builders fixed
the ceiling and put up new beams. They patched crumbling
walls with new stones.

In the temple, Hilkiah the priest found a scroll—a
book on rolled-up paper. "What's this?" he wondered.
He brushed off the dust and dirt. "Moses wrote this long
ago," he said. "These are God's words to us!"

Hilkiah gave the scroll to King Josiah's helper, who read
it to the king.

"I feel so sad!" King Josiah cried. "We and our parents
and grandparents have not obeyed God's Word! We have
not been doing what this scroll says we should do."

King Josiah called all the people to meet him at the
temple. He read the words on the scroll for everyone
to hear.

"We're glad to hear the words of God!" the people
said. They promised to obey God from then on, and God
brought peace to their land.

God never changes, and His words don't change. It doesn't matter whether we read God's words in the morning, at lunchtime, at bedtime, or sometime in between—God's words are always the same, and they are always true. The Bible, God's Word, tells us how much God loves us and how we can love Him back by obeying His Word.

- When you listen to Mom or Dad or a teacher but don't obey, what happens?

- What is your favorite story from the Bible? Why?

> Dear God, thank You for the Bible. Please help me always want to listen to Your Word and learn more about Your love. Amen.

Ask a grown-up to help you make a scroll. Find two unsharpened pencils, a sheet of paper, and some tape. Cut the width of the paper to one inch less than the length of the pencils. Turn the paper the long way. Tape one pencil to each end of the paper. Roll both pencils toward the middle of the paper. When your scroll is complete, unroll it and write on it Psalm 119:57 (today's Bible verse).

· · • • ● ● • • ·

REMEMBER
God's Word never changes.

I have promised to obey your words.

—PSALM 119:57 ICB

GOOD JOB!

ESTHER 1–10

Beautiful Esther lived in Susa, a royal city of Persia. The king of Persia chose Esther to be his queen.

The king had a helper named Haman. Everyone was supposed to bow down to Haman whenever he rode by. But Esther's cousin, Mordecai, would not bow down to Haman. Mordecai, a Jew, would bow down only to God. Haman hated Mordecai—and all the Jewish people—because of this.

So Haman asked the king to make a law: on a certain day, the people of the Persian empire should kill all the Jews who lived throughout the kingdom! The king agreed—but he didn't know Esther was Jewish!

Mordecai told Esther to go to the king and ask him to save the Jewish people.

"But no one is supposed to go to the king without being asked," Esther said. "Unless he holds out his golden scepter, it's dangerous."

"Maybe you became queen **for just a time like this**," Mordecai said, "when you can help your people."

Esther thought about that. "I will fast for three days to get ready," she said. "Then I will go to see the king."

The king welcomed Esther by holding out his golden scepter. When he heard what Esther had to say, he was angry with Haman, and he made a new law: the Jewish people could fight and defend themselves. And thanks to Esther, they did.

God gives everyone talents and abilities. We all are good at different things, and we all have different jobs. But everyone can serve God and help other people!

- What are some things you enjoy doing or are really good at? How could you serve God with those talents or abilities?

- What are some things you do every day? How can you help others while you do those things?

> Dear God, thank You for giving everyone a way to serve You. Help me serve You with all the things I do. Amen.

With your family or friends, act out Esther's story. Choose someone to be the king, Esther, Haman, and Mordecai. You might want to make some paper crowns and a golden scepter to use as props.

• • • ● ● ● • • •

REMEMBER
God gives everyone abilities for serving Him.

Work as if you were working for the Lord.

—COLOSSIANS 3:23 ICB

FOUR IN THE FIRE

DANIEL 3

King Nebuchadnezzar made a tall golden statue. "When the music plays," said King Neb, "everyone must bow down and worship the statue."

Horns tooted. Flutes fluted. Harps hummed. All the people bowed—except Shadrach, Meshach, and Abednego.

"King Neb!" some of the king's helpers cried. "Three young men have disobeyed your law!"

"Is this true?" King Neb roared. "Bow down to my statue, or I will throw you into the fiery furnace."

But Shadrach, Meshach, and Abednego said, "Our God can rescue us! But no matter what, we will not worship your gods or your golden statue."

"Make the furnace hotter than hot!" the king yelled. **Crackle, crackle!** Into the flames went Shadrach, Meshach, and Abednego.

"Look!" the king said. "We put three men in the furnace, but now there are four!" God had sent help to Shadrach, Meshach, and Abednego! He kept them safe.

"Come out!" the king yelled. Shadrach, Meshach, and Abednego came out. They were not burned at all.

"Praise to the God of Shadrach, Meshach, and Abednego!" the king said. "Only He can rescue like this!"

God watches over us and wants us to make good choices to stay safe, like holding Mom or Dad's hand in a parking lot and wearing a helmet when we ride our bikes. And sometimes God rescues us from trouble to keep us safe. Shadrach, Meshach, and Abednego trusted God to take care of them, no matter what happened. We can too!

- **What are some of your family's rules for staying safe?**

- **Why does God watch over us and take care of us?**

> Dear God, thank You for loving us and taking care of us. Thank You for keeping us safe. Amen.

God worked a miracle for Shadrach, Meshach, and Abednego in the fire. But God keeps us safe from fire by helping us learn safety rules. Talk with a grown-up about fire safety. Help your family make a fire safety plan. Then draw a picture of your plan.

• • • ● ● ● • • •

REMEMBER
God watches over us.

Keep me safe, O God.

—Psalm 16:1 NLT

DANIEL FOR DINNER?

DANIEL 6

The king of Babylon made a law that people could pray only to him. But Daniel loved God and prayed only to God.

"Daniel won't obey the king's law," said some of the king's helpers. "Throw him into the lions' den!"

The king liked Daniel. "I am sorry about the law I made," he said. He tried to find a way to save Daniel.

But the law was the law. The king's helpers picked Daniel up and threw him into the den of hungry lions with a **thud**. "May your God rescue you!" the king shouted to Daniel.

That night the king could not eat or sleep. In the morning he hurried to the lions' den.

"Daniel?" called the king.

"Hello, King!" Daniel called back. "I am just fine! God sent an angel to close the mouths of the hungry lions. They did not hurt me."

"Everyone must worship Daniel's God," the king said. "He works mighty miracles!"

THINK AND TALK

Prayer is talking with God. Daniel loved God and loved to talk to Him. He didn't let anything stop him from praying. We can talk with God just like Daniel did! And when we talk to Him, God listens!

- Who is your favorite person to talk with? What do you talk about?

- When do you talk with God? What do you talk with God about?

> Dear God, I love You, and I love to talk with You. Amen!

Get a paper plate, some yarn and glue, and a few crayons or markers. Draw the face of a lion on the paper plate. Add some yarn for the lion's mane. Ask a grown-up to print "Remember to Pray" around the bottom of the plate. Put the lion in your room to remind you to pray to God, just as Daniel did.

· · ● ● ● ● · · ·

REMEMBER
God hears our prayers.

Hear me when I call, O God.

—Psalm 4:1 KJV

SWIMMING WITH A BIG FISH

JONAH 1-3

Go to Nineveh," God told Jonah. "Warn the people. Everything they do is bad."

But Jonah didn't like the Ninevites, so he ran the other way. He found a ship, bought a ticket, and went on board.

He thought he could get away from God.

Whoosh! God sent a powerful wind over the sea. Huge waves pounded the ship. The sailors thought the ship would break into pieces. "Why is this happening?" they cried.

"It's my fault," Jonah said. "Throw me into the sea, and the storm will stop."

Splash! Jonah sank into the sea. Then God sent a big fish to swallow Jonah to save him. **Gulp!**

Inside the fish, Jonah prayed. "Oh, God," he said. "Please help me, and I will praise You. You are the only One who can save me." After three days, God told the fish to spit Jonah out onto dry land. **Burp!**

"Go to Nineveh," God told Jonah again.

This time Jonah obeyed. He went to Nineveh and gave God's message to the king and the people. And they listened! They asked God to forgive them for the wrong things they had done, and they started doing what is right.

God wants us to love Him and to love other people. He wants us to think about what others need and help them. He wants us to tell others that He loves them. The people of Nineveh needed Jonah to come and talk to them and give them God's message. When Jonah obeyed God, good things happened!

- God wants us to be kind to others. How could you show kindness to someone today?

- God wants us to tell others about Him. What are some ways you do that in your family?

Dear God, help me obey what You say, even if it's hard. Help me tell others how good You are! Amen.

Jonah needed a loud voice to give God's message to the people of Nineveh. Make a megaphone so your voice will be louder. Wash an empty plastic milk jug and let it dry. Ask a grown-up to carefully cut off the bottom. Decorate the milk jug using crayons, markers, and stickers or using glue and colored paper. Then hold the handle with one hand and talk into the spout.

• • ●●●●●• ••

REMEMBER
God wants everyone to know Him.

Every day tell how he saves us.

—1 Chronicles 16:23 ICB

NEW TESTAMENT STORIES

BIG NIGHT IN A LITTLE TOWN

LUKE 2

Crackle! Hiss! A campfire sizzled. Sheep snuggled nearby, cozy and warm. Sleepy shepherds guarded their sheep under the dark night sky.

Suddenly an angel appeared, shining brightly. "Don't be afraid!" the angel's big voice boomed. "I have good news for you and all people! A special baby has been born! He is the Savior, the One God promised to send! You will find Him wrapped in swaddling clothes and lying in a manger."

Then all the angels of heaven filled the sky. "Glory to God!" they said. "Peace on earth!"

The angels disappeared. "**Let's go!**" said the shepherds. "Let's find the baby the angel told us about."

In Bethlehem the shepherds found Mary and Joseph and the brand-new baby, Jesus. He was wrapped in swaddling clothes and lying in a manger. "It's Him!" the shepherds said. "Just like the angel told us! This baby is Jesus, God's Son!"

Shepherds got dirty and smelly taking care of their sheep, and other people often didn't want them around. But God wanted everyone, even stinky shepherds, to know that Jesus was born! God had promised Someone would come to make things right again, and now that Someone had arrived! The good news the angel gave the shepherds was the best news they would ever hear. It's the best news for us today too—Jesus, the Savior, has come!

- How do you feel when someone tells you good news?

- How do you think the shepherds felt when they saw baby Jesus?

> Dear God, thank You for sending our Savior, Jesus. Help me tell others the good news that He has come! Amen.

Ask a grown-up to show you how to swaddle a baby. (You can use a baby doll.) Pretend to be the shepherds worshipping baby Jesus in the stable. Sing this lullaby to the baby to the tune of "Are You Sleeping?":

Baby Jesus, Baby Jesus,
God's dear Son, God's dear Son,
We are glad to see You! We are glad to meet You!
Go to sleep. Go to sleep.

REMEMBER
Jesus is God's Son.

The Father sent his Son to be the Savior of the world.

—1 JOHN 4:14 ICB

TALLER AND WISER

MATTHEW 2; MARK 6; LUKE 2

Jesus didn't stay a tiny baby. He grew! Wise men from the east came to Bethlehem to worship Him when He was a toddler. Then Joseph and Mary took Him to Egypt for a while to keep Him safe from a mean king named Herod. After Herod died, when Jesus was a bigger boy, His family came back to live in the town of Nazareth.

In Nazareth, Joseph worked as a carpenter, making things out of wood. As Jesus grew up, He learned to be a carpenter too. **Hammer, hammer. Saw, saw, saw!**

When He was twelve, Jesus went with Mary and Joseph to Jerusalem to worship at the temple. Jesus found the temple teachers and spent time talking with them and asking them questions. They asked Him questions too, and they were amazed by all He understood. Mary and Joseph thought Jesus was lost, and they searched all over the city for Him. When they found Him, Jesus asked, "Didn't you know I had to be in My Father's house?"

Jesus kept growing taller and wiser. He obeyed Mary and Joseph. He learned to read, and He memorized God's Word. He treated people kindly and with respect. God was pleased with Him, and people were too.

THINK AND TALK

Jesus grew from a baby to a boy to a man. He grew in stature. (That means He got taller and stronger.) And He grew in wisdom. (Having wisdom means knowing what God says is good and true.) Growing is God's plan! You are growing too.

- What are some ways you are growing physically? What helps you grow?

- What are some ways you are growing wiser? What helps you grow? How are you using your wisdom?

> Dear God, thank You that I'm growing and learning every day. Help me to please You and other people as I grow. Amen.

Ask Mom or Dad to help you find photos of yourself as a baby and photos that show how you have grown. You might want to print some out and use them to make a poster.

• • • ● ● ● ● • •

REMEMBER
Jesus grew.

The child grew and became strong.

—LUKE 2:40 NIV

TOO MANY FISH

LUKE 5

Jesus grew up. He began to preach and teach. One day He sat in Peter's boat and taught the people sitting on the beach.

Then Jesus said, "Peter, let's go fishing. Take the boat out to deeper water. Let down your nets to catch some fish."

"We fished all night and didn't catch one fish," Peter said. "But if You say so, OK. I will do it."

Peter rowed the boat out to deeper water. He threw the heavy nets into the water. Down, down they went. Suddenly . . .

Swish! Swoosh! Flopping, plopping fish filled Peter's nets. **Splish! Splash!** "Help!" Peter yelled. "I've caught too many fish! The boat is going to sink!"

James and John rowed out to help. The fish filled up their boat too!

Where had this great catch of fish come from? Peter and the others looked at Jesus.

"Don't be afraid," Jesus said. "From now on you will be fishing for people." The men left everything behind and followed Jesus.

Jesus can do anything! He can make fish fill the water for fishermen's nets. And just as the fishermen caught a lot of fish, Jesus wants us to "catch" a lot of people by helping them know, love, and follow Him every day. If *we* follow Jesus, He will help us do just that!

- Have you ever gone fishing? Did you use a fishing pole or a net?

- Have you ever told anyone "Jesus loves you"? Who is someone you could tell today?

> Dear God, I want to follow Jesus and "fish" for people so they can love and follow Him too! Amen.

Make paper footprints, right and left, by tracing around a grown-up's shoes. You can use colored paper and a crayon to trace the footprints; then cut them out. Make a footprint trail around the house and follow it. Jesus wants us to follow Him!

· • ● ● ● ● • ·

REMEMBER
Jesus leads us.

Follow in his steps.
—1 Peter 2:21 NLT

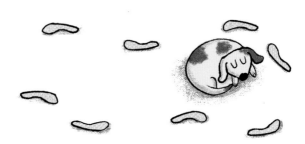

THROUGH THE ROOF

MARK 2; LUKE 5

A man who couldn't walk lay on a mat. Four friends carried him to see Jesus.

"Here's the house where Jesus is," the four friends said. "Hold on. We're going in."

But they couldn't even get near the door! There were too many people.

"Hold on!" the four friends said. "We're going up!" **Clomp, clomp, clomp!** They carried the man up the stairs to the roof, which was flat.

The four friends made a hole in the roof. "Hold on!" they said. "You're going down!" They let the man down through the hole in the roof. Right in front of Jesus!

Jesus looked at the man and said, "My friend, your sins are forgiven. Stand up, pick up your mat, and go home!"

The man stood up! He could run! He could jump! He picked up his mat and walked through the crowd. Amazed, all the people praised God and said, "We've never seen anything like this before!"

THINK AND TALK

Sometimes our bodies need healing. Sometimes we need healing in our hearts and minds because we have sinned. Jesus has power to heal our bodies and power to forgive sins because He is God. There is no one else like Jesus, and nothing is too hard for Him.

- What is something hard for you to do? Do you ask Jesus for help when you need it?

- What should you do when you know you have done something wrong?

> Dear God, thank You for Jesus' power to forgive us and heal us, inside and out. Thank You for all the wonderful things He can do! Amen.

Do ten things that use your legs. Here are ideas to get you started. Can you walk? Run? Jump? March? Hop? Skip? Dance? Stand on your tiptoes? Ride a bike? Climb a jungle gym? What else can you do?

• • ◦ ● ● ◦ • •

REMEMBER
Jesus can heal us inside and out.

[Jesus] alone has the power to save.

—James 4:12 NLT

WIND AND WAVES OBEY HIM

MARK 4; LUKE 8

Let's cross over to the other side of the lake," Jesus told the disciples—His twelve special followers. So they all got in a boat.

Jesus felt tired and wanted to nap. He put His head on a cushion at the back of the boat and fell asleep.

Then a fierce storm came down on the lake, but Jesus kept on sleeping. **Whish! Whoosh!** The wind blew hard and strong. **Slap! Slam!** Huge waves crashed over the boat.

"We're sinking!" the disciples yelled. They went to Jesus and woke Him up. "Jesus!" they shouted. "Don't You care that we're going to drown?"

Jesus saw the storm. "Quiet!" He told the wind. The wind stopped blowing. "Be still!" He told the waves. The waves stopped crashing.

Jesus looked at His disciples. "Why were you afraid?" He asked.

Jesus' disciples didn't know what to say. They had never known anyone like Jesus. "Even the wind and the waves obey Him!" they said to one another.

THINK AND TALK

Jesus knew just what to do when the disciples were afraid during the storm, and He had power to help them. Jesus knows just what to do when things scare us or when we're worried about what's happening around us. The disciples asked Jesus to help them, and He did. He will help us too whenever we ask Him.

- What kinds of things worry you? What are you afraid of?

- What would you like to ask Jesus to help you with today?

> Dear Jesus, thank You for Your strong power to help when I am worried or afraid. Amen.

Make a boat on the floor with cushions or a big box. Sing these words to the tune of "Row, Row, Row Your Boat" as you pretend to row across the sea with Jesus:

> Row, row, row your boat
> On the stormy sea.
> Jesus calmed the wind and waves,
> And He'll take care of me!

• • • ● ● ● ● • • •

REMEMBER
Jesus' power can calm any storm.

All power is his forever and ever.

—1 PETER 5:11 ICB

FEEDING HUNGRY PEOPLE

MARK 6; LUKE 9

People who had been listening to Jesus all day rubbed their hungry tummies. **Rumble, grumble!**

"It's getting late," said Jesus' disciples. "Let's send the people away so they can buy food."

"We don't have to send them away," Jesus said. "You can feed them."

"There are too many people!" the disciples said. "We have only five loaves of bread and two small fish, a young boy's lunch."

"Tell the people to sit down in groups on the grass," Jesus said. He thanked God for the bread and fish. He broke the bread into pieces for the disciples to give to the people. He did the same thing with the fish.

Jesus made just five loaves of bread and two little fish feed the big crowd! All the people ate as much as they wanted. One young boy's lunch was enough for everyone, and the leftovers filled twelve baskets!

THINK AND TALK

Jesus made just a little food turn into enough for everyone in the crowd to have plenty to eat! He always knows just what we need, and He will take care of us and give us what we need at just the right time.

- What are some things that you need every day?

- What are some of the ways God provides food for us?

> Dear God, thank You for always caring about us and giving us what we need. Amen.

Make a picture list. On a sheet of paper, draw pictures of everything you ate today. Thank God for giving you the food you need every day.

• • • ● ● ● • • •

REMEMBER
Jesus gives us what we need.

"Give us the food we need for each day."

—Matthew 6:11 ICB

HOW TO BE A NEIGHBOR

LUKE 10

One of God's laws is "Love your neighbor as yourself." A scribe (a Jewish teacher) asked Jesus, "But who *is* my neighbor?" So Jesus told him this story:

A Jewish man traveling on the road to Jericho was stopped by robbers. They took his clothes, beat him up, and left him by the side of the road.

Soon a priest came along. He knew God's law about loving your neighbor, but when he saw the hurt man lying there, he crossed over to the other side of the road and walked on by.

Next a temple worker came along. He knew God's law too. He walked over to look at the hurt man, but he also crossed over to the other side of the road and walked on by.

Then a Samaritan came along. (The Jewish people did *not* like Samaritans.) When he saw the hurt man, he felt sorry for him, and he stopped to help. He cleaned and bandaged the man's wounds and put the man on his own donkey. **Clip-clop, clip-clop.** The Samaritan took the man to an inn and cared for him there. The next day he gave the innkeeper money and said, "Take care of this man. If you spend more than this to help him, I will pay you back the next time I'm here."

Jesus looked at the scribe and asked, "Now which of the three men was a neighbor to the man attacked by robbers?"

"The one who was kind to him," the scribe replied.

"Yes," Jesus said. "Now go and do the same."

Jesus wants us to be good neighbors to all people, helping them and showing them kindness and love whenever we can. We should treat other people the way we would like to be treated—that's Jesus' golden rule.

- How has someone been a good neighbor to you?

- Who are some people who might need you to be a good neighbor to them—at school, at church, or in your community? How can you show them kindness and love?

> Dear God, help me be a good neighbor whenever I can. Show me who needs my help. Amen.

Make a Good Samaritan bag and be ready to help someone. Fill a quart-sized plastic bag with a water bottle, snack bars, chewing gum, wet wipes, a toothbrush, toothpaste, and perhaps a gift card to a restaurant or gas station. Keep the bag in the family car and give it to someone in need.

· • •● ●● •● •● • ·

REMEMBER
Jesus wants us to be good neighbors.

Always try to do good . . . to all people.

—1 Thessalonians 5:15 nlt

BUSY MARTHA

LUKE 10

Work, work, work! So much to do! Dinner for Jesus must be *just* right.

Sweep the floor. Set the table. Run to the market and home again. Roast the meat. Cook the vegetables. **Bubble, bubble!** Boil the grain! Hurry, hurry, *hurry!*

Suddenly Martha stopped. She wiped her forehead and pushed back her hair. "Mary should be helping me," Martha said. *Where was her sister, Mary?*

Martha stepped out of the kitchen and looked around. Jesus sat in the living room, teaching about God. Mary sat at His feet, listening to every word.

Martha put her hands on her hips. "Jesus!" she said. "This isn't fair! My sister just sits there while I do all the work! Tell her to come and help me."

"My dear Martha," Jesus said kindly. "You are fussing about so many details! Only one thing is so important. Mary has found it, and she will never lose it. She is spending time with Me."

THINK AND TALK

No matter how much fun we will have today, spending time with Jesus is the best and most important thing we can do. Jesus loves us and wants us to spend time with Him, listening to what He has to say and what He wants to teach us. Where do we find those words? In the Bible!

- What are some of your favorite things to do?

- What's the best time of day for you and your family to listen to Jesus' words?

> Dear God, thank You that I can listen to Jesus whenever I read Your Word, the Bible. Help me do that every day. Amen.

Ask a grown-up if there's a red-letter Bible at your house, or plan a visit to a bookstore and look at one there. Flip through some of the pages in Matthew, Mark, Luke, and John, and you can see some of the words Jesus spoke on earth printed in red ink! Wow! That's a lot of important words!

• • ● ● ● ● • •

REMEMBER
Jesus teaches us.

Let the teaching of Christ live in you.
—Colossians 3:16 ICB

LAZARUS, COME OUT!

JOHN 11

Jesus came to the village of Bethany. His friend Lazarus had died.

"If You had been here," said Martha and Mary, "our brother would not have died."

"Where have you put his body?" Jesus asked.

"Come and see," said Mary and Martha and Lazarus's friends.

They took Jesus to a cave shut tight with a large stone.

Jesus cried. Then He said, "Move the stone away."

"But the smell will be terrible!" Martha said.

"If you believe, you will see how amazing God is," Jesus said. So they rolled the stone away.

Jesus looked up to heaven and talked to God. "Thank You for hearing Me," He said. "May everyone here know that You sent Me." Then Jesus shouted, "**Lazarus, come out!**"

Lazarus walked out of the cave, alive again! "Take off the grave clothes and let him go!" Jesus said.

When autumn comes, leaves turn brown and fall to the ground. You might see ladybugs or beetles that aren't moving. They died. Something dead doesn't come back to life again—but Lazarus did! Jesus made Lazarus alive again to show everyone His power over life and death. And everyone who believes in Jesus will live again in heaven someday.

- When someone you love goes on a trip or visits you and then goes back home, how do you feel?

- How do you think Mary and Martha felt when Lazarus was alive again?

> Dear God, I'm so glad Jesus has power over life and death. Thank You that we can live forever with You in heaven because of Jesus. Amen.

Sing these words to the tune of "Three Blind Mice." If you don't know the tune, say the words aloud like a chant.

Lazarus! Lazarus!
Come out now! Come out now!
Jesus has power over everything!
Even dead people can rise and sing.
This is the reason that Jesus is King!
Thank You, God!

• • ● ● ● ● ● • •

REMEMBER
Jesus gives life.

"Whoever believes has eternal life."

—John 6:47 ESV

ONLY ONE?

LUKE 17

Jesus walked from place to place, teaching about God and healing people who were sick. In one village **10** men were sick with leprosy, a terrible skin disease. People with leprosy had to stay far away from others.

The **10** lepers saw Jesus and began calling, "Jesus, have mercy on us!"

Jesus saw the lepers. "Go and show yourselves to the priests," He said. That was the rule for people who were healed.

But the lepers weren't healed yet. What would they do? **1–2–3–4–5–6–7–8–9–10** men started down the road to see the priests. As they went, they were healed. Their leprosy was gone!

1–2–3–4–5–6–7–8–9 men kept on going to see the priests. But **1** man turned around and hurried back to Jesus, shouting, "Praise God!" He bowed down at Jesus' feet and thanked Him for making him well. And this man, the **1** who came back to thank Jesus, was a Samaritan.

"Didn't I heal **10** men?" asked Jesus. "Where are the other **9**? Only this foreigner came back to praise God?"

"Stand up and go," Jesus told the Samaritan. "Your faith has saved you."

THINK AND TALK

It's polite to say please and thank you, but Jesus wants us to be more than polite. He wants us to be thankful in our hearts. When we are thankful, we give God glory and show other people how good He is.

- What are some things you are thankful God has given you or done for you?

- If you were one of the ten healed men, would you have turned back as the Samaritan did, or would you have kept going?

> Dear God, thank You for loving me, taking care of me, and teaching me. Help me to always be thankful. Amen.

Sing "If You're Happy and You Know It," substituting the word *thankful* for *happy* and doing the motions.

If you're thankful and you know it, clap your hands.
If you're thankful and you know it, clap your hands.
If you're thankful and you know it, then
you really want to show it.
If you're thankful and you know it, clap your hands.

• • ● ● ● ● • •

REMEMBER
Jesus wants us to be thankful.

Give thanks to the LORD.

—PSALM 118:1 ESV

NEVER TOO BUSY

MATTHEW 19; MARK 10

Babies squealed in their mothers' arms. Boys and girls skipped and hopped along the path. Soon they would see Jesus!

"There He is!" someone shouted.

"**Stop!**" said Jesus' disciples to the children and the mothers and fathers. "Don't go any farther."

"Please, sir," one mother said. "We want to see Jesus. We want Him to give our children a blessing."

"Jesus is busy," the disciples scolded. "He doesn't have time for children."

Jesus heard what the disciples said. "**Stop!**" Jesus told them. "Let the children come to Me. Never send them away. I am never too busy for children. In My kingdom, children are very important! Everyone must enter My kingdom with faith like a little child's."

The children smiled. The mothers and fathers smiled. The disciples stepped aside, and the children ran to Jesus. He took them in His arms. He put His hands on their heads and blessed them. He held the babies and blessed them too. Then He went on His way.

What a happy day!

THINK AND TALK

Jesus was glad to see the children, and He was happy to stop what He was doing to talk with them and bless them. He cared about them, and He cares about you and all children everywhere too. He wants you to talk with Him— and He always listens—because He loves you so much!

- How would it feel to be one of the children who spent time with Jesus that day?

- How does it feel to know that Jesus cares about you and wants to spend time with you too?

> Dear God, thank You for my friend Jesus! I'm so glad He cares about me! Amen.

Parents and caregivers, you can bless your children with special prayers for them. Here's an example to get you started, adapted from Ephesians 1:15–20: "May you grow strong in faith, love, and wisdom, knowing God well. May your heart be full of His light, leading you on His path with confidence and hope. May you always experience God's mighty power that is given to those who believe in Jesus Christ." Try praying a blessing over your child every day or every night at bedtime.

• • • • • • • •

REMEMBER
Jesus loves you!

"Let the little children come to me."

—MATTHEW 19:14 ICB

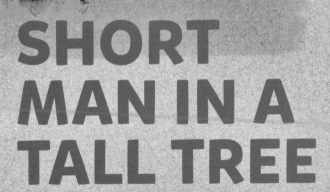

SHORT MAN IN A TALL TREE

LUKE 19

lease let me see. I want to see Jesus too!" Zacchaeus stood on tiptoe, but he was too short to see over the crowd at the side of the road.

So Zacchaeus ran ahead and climbed a tree. And just in time, because Jesus was coming his way.

Jesus looked up and saw Zacchaeus in the tree. "Come down, Zacchaeus! I need to eat at your house today!"

He knows my name! Zacchaeus sprang out of the tree and took Jesus home for dinner.

The people complained. **Grumble, grumble!** Zacchaeus was a tax collector, and tax collectors cheated people. Why did Jesus want to stay with *him*?

But Zacchaeus decided to stop cheating!

"Lord, I will give away half of everything I own!" Zacchaeus said. "And if I cheated anyone, I will give him back four times as much!"

"Zacchaeus has faith in Me now," Jesus said. "I came to find and save everyone like him."

THINK AND TALK

Jesus knew Zacchaeus was a tax collector who cheated people, but He loved and cared about Zacchaeus just the same. He wanted Zacchaeus to believe in Him and live right, and Zacchaeus decided he wanted that too!

- What do you think Jesus and Zacchaeus talked about while they ate together?

- How do we know what things are right and good? When have you done something because it was right?

> Dear God, thank You for loving us even when we do wrong. Thank You for sending Jesus for us. Amen.

Zacchaeus went looking for Jesus, and Jesus was looking for him! Play a game of hide-and-seek with a friend or a grown-up.

· · ● ● ◉ ● ● · ·

REMEMBER
Jesus wants us to do right.

Jesus went everywhere doing good.

—Acts 10:38 ICB

PARADE FOR A KING

MATTHEW 21; MARK 11; LUKE 19; JOHN 12

Jesus walked with His disciples toward the big city of Jerusalem for the Passover feast.

Two disciples found a young donkey for Jesus to ride on. They threw their coats over the donkey. Then Jesus sat on it and rode toward the city. **Clip-clop, clip-clop.**

People going to the city filled the road and walked along with Jesus. People in the city heard that Jesus was coming. "Let's go out to meet Him!" they said.

When the people saw Jesus, some spread their coats on the road. Some spread palm branches from the fields. Coats and branches made a colorful path for Jesus to ride on.

Jesus' followers surrounded Him as He rode along. They sang and praised God with loud voices. "Praise God!" they said. "Blessed is the King who comes in the name of the Lord!"

The parade for Jesus came into Jerusalem. The whole city noticed. "Who is this?" people asked.

The crowds answered, "This is Jesus, the King!"

A good king takes care of the people in his kingdom. He keeps them safe and shows them how to live. Jesus loves us and takes care of us. He keeps us safe and shows us how to live. God has a kingdom, and He sent Jesus to be our very good King!

- One of King Jesus' rules is "Love God." What is a way you show you love God?

- Jesus' other rule is "Love people." What is a way you show love to others?

> Dear God, thank You for King Jesus! Help me always love and praise Him. Amen.

Pretend you are going to Jerusalem with Jesus and have a parade. Some friends can ride on riding toys. You might play rhythm instruments, like a drum or cymbals, too. Sing a praise song as you parade around your house or neighborhood.

• • • ● ● ● • •

REMEMBER
Jesus is our King.

He is Jesus Christ our Lord.

—ROMANS 1:4 NLT

GLAD GIVER

MARK 12; LUKE 21

At the temple Jesus sat down to watch the people giving offerings.

Some very rich people put lots of their money in the offering box.

PLINK, PLINK!

CLATTER, CLATTER!

PLINK!

And even though these people gave so much money, they still had plenty of money left.

Then a woman came to give an offering. Her husband had died, and she had hardly any money at all. Jesus watched as this woman dropped two tiny coins into the offering box.

Plink, plink.

Jesus called His disciples to Him. "This woman gave more than all those rich people," He said. "They have so much and still have much left over. She gave everything she had to live on."

We give offerings to thank God for everything He's given to us. God wants us to be glad givers. Giving with a thankful heart is more important than whether we have a lot or a little to give.

- Does your family give an offering at church? What does your church do with the offerings you give?

- Sometimes we don't have any money. What are some other things you could give to help someone else?

> Dear God, thank You for all the good things You do for us! Help me give gladly with a thankful heart. Amen.

Make a "bank" for your room. Ask Mom or Dad for three plastic containers with lids. With a permanent marker, label one container "Give," another container "Save," and the third container "Spend." Whenever you receive money for chores or as a gift, divide it up among the three containers.

• • ● ● ● • • •

REMEMBER
Jesus wants us to give gladly.

God loves a cheerful giver.

—2 Corinthians 9:7 esv

THE SADDEST DAY

MATTHEW 27; MARK 15

Jesus' followers couldn't understand what was happening. At the top of a hill, soldiers nailed Jesus' feet and hands to a heavy wooden cross!

Jesus had never done anything wrong, but He knew the cross was why He came to earth. God had planned for His own Son to die for the sins of the whole world.

"Father, forgive them," Jesus said. "These people don't know what they are doing."

At noon, the sky went dark. At three o'clock, Jesus called out to God, and then He died. **Roar! Rumble!** The earth shook. Rocks split apart.

"Surely this man was the Son of God!" said one of the soldiers at the cross.

A man named Joseph took Jesus' body down from the cross. He wrapped it in linen cloths and laid it in a tomb in a rocky place. He closed up the tomb with a big stone.

Soldiers guarded the tomb. Jesus had said that after He died, He would rise again on the third day. But some people didn't believe Him.

Jesus could have come down from the cross, but He stayed there because He loves us. Jesus never did even one wrong thing, but He died for the wrong things we do so someday we can live with Him in heaven forever! It was God's plan to save us from our sin. It is the way God planned for Jesus to make everything right again. Now He wants us to believe in Jesus and thank Him for what He did for us.

- Jesus said He would rise again on the third day. Do you think He did? (See the next story if you're not sure.)

- What are sins? Do you ever sin?

Dear God, thank You for sending Jesus to save us. I love Him. Amen.

Find two craft sticks or two paint stirrers. Write *JESUS* across one stick and *SAVES* down the other. Glue the sticks together like a cross, with the *S* in the middle of *JESUS* overlapping the *S* at the beginning of *SAVES*. Draw a little crown at the top of the cross.

· · • • ● ▶ • • · ·

REMEMBER
Jesus saves us.

Christ died for our sins.

—1 Corinthians 15:3 icb

GOOD NEWS!

MATTHEW 28; MARK 16; LUKE 24

Early Sunday morning, just as the sun began to shine, some of the women who followed Jesus walked to Jesus' tomb, feeling so sad because Jesus had died.

Suddenly a big earthquake shook the ground. **Rumble! Rumble!**

An angel came down from heaven, rolled away the stone, and sat on it. The guards outside the tomb fainted when they saw the angel.

The women looked inside the tomb. Jesus' body wasn't there! Then two angels stood beside them.

"Don't be afraid," the angels said. "You are looking for Jesus. He isn't here! He has risen from the dead, just as He said! Come, see the place where His body was lying. Now go quickly and tell His disciples the news!"

The women turned and ran with joyful hearts. On the way, they saw Jesus! They ran to Him and worshipped Him.

"Don't be afraid," He said. "Go and tell My disciples to meet Me in Galilee. I will see them there."

THINK AND TALK

Jesus promised He would rise again on the third day, and He did! The happy, surprised women who saw Him alive again couldn't wait to tell His friends the good news! Everyone needs to hear that Jesus died and rose again. It's really good news!

- 🪁 **When is a time you felt surprised or happy?**

- 🪁 **Is there someone you could tell the good news about Jesus today?**

> Dear God, I'm happy that Jesus is alive! Thank You for this really good news! Amen.

Easter is a special time to celebrate that Jesus is alive again. Flowers, colored eggs, baby chicks, and bunnies help us think about new life. But we can celebrate Easter and new life all year long. Plant some peas or beans in your yard or in a container. Be sure to water the seeds and make sure they have plenty of sunshine. Then watch them grow! From just a little seed comes a living plant!

REMEMBER
Jesus is alive!

God raised Jesus from the dead.

—ACTS 2:32 NLT

BREAKFAST ON THE BEACH

JOHN 21

On the night before Jesus died, Peter felt afraid and acted like he didn't know Jesus—three different times! Peter knew that was wrong, and he wondered if Jesus would forgive him for what he had done.

"I'm going fishing," Peter said one night after Jesus had risen.

"We'll come too," said some of the other disciples. Peter and John and their friends fished all night, but they didn't catch any fish.

In the morning, they saw a man standing on the shore. "Throw in your nets to the right of the boat," He called. The nets filled up with fish!

"It's Jesus!" John said.

Peter jumped into the water and swam to the shore. Over a campfire, Jesus had cooked fish and bread for His friends. **Sizzle! Pop!** "Come and have breakfast," Jesus said.

When they all had finished eating, Jesus asked, "Peter, do you love Me?" Jesus asked this question three times, and three times Peter answered, "You know I do, Lord."

"Feed My sheep and follow Me!" Jesus told him.

Peter knew he was forgiven, and Jesus had work for him to do!

THINK AND TALK

Everyone needs forgiveness because everyone sins and makes mistakes. God is glad to forgive us because Jesus took our punishment when He died on the cross. Being forgiven gives us a new start—every day!

- What is forgiveness?

- How do you think Peter felt when Jesus forgave him?

> Dear God, thank You for forgiveness, and thank You for Jesus! Amen.

Have a backyard breakfast of bread and fish sticks with your family. Talk about what forgiveness means to you.

REMEMBER
Jesus forgives us.

God through Christ has forgiven you.

—EPHESIANS 4:32 NLT

RIDE ON A CLOUD

LUKE 24; ACTS 1

Forty days after He arose, Jesus led His disciples to a hill called the Mount of Olives. Soon He would leave His friends and return to heaven.

"Wait in the city for the Holy Spirit to come," He said. "You will receive power. Then tell people everywhere about Me."

As Jesus prayed for His disciples, a cloud surrounded Him and carried Him up to heaven.

The disciples stretched their necks and stared into the sky as hard as they could, until they couldn't see Jesus anymore.

Suddenly two men in white robes appeared. "Why are you standing here staring into the sky?" they asked. "Jesus has been taken from you into heaven. But listen to this! Someday He will come back! Yes, Jesus will come back riding on a cloud, just the way you saw Him go!"

The disciples worshipped Jesus. They would miss Him, but their hearts beat joyfully just the same. **Thump-thump, thump-thump!** They went back to Jerusalem and waited, just as Jesus had told them to do.

THINK AND TALK

When a holiday is over or a special visit ends, we feel sad, but we look forward to the next time we'll celebrate that holiday or spend time with our friends. Even though Jesus has gone back to heaven, we can look forward to the day He comes to earth again. And we can obey Him now while we are waiting for that day!

- Who is a friend or relative whose visits you look forward to? What makes those visits special?

- What are some ways you obey Jesus now while we wait for Him to return?

> Dear God, I'm glad Jesus will come back to earth someday! Help me obey Him while I wait. Amen.

GREEN MEANS GO!

Play a cloud-watching game with a friend or a grown-up. Go outside and look up at the clouds. Lie on your back if you can. Find clouds with shapes that look like something else. Take turns. Say, "I spy a cloud that looks like _____. Can you find it?"

. • •◉●◉●• •.

REMEMBER
Jesus will come back.

We are waiting for our Savior, the Lord Jesus Christ, to come from heaven.

—Philippians 3:20 ICB

THE HOLY SPIRIT COMES

ACTS 2

After Jesus went back to heaven, His disciples stayed together in a house in Jerusalem. Suddenly— **Whoosh! Roar!** A sound like a mighty windstorm filled the room. **Flicker! Flash!** Flames of fire danced above each person's head.

God had sent the Holy Spirit!

The Spirit filled all the people who believed in Jesus. They began to speak in languages they didn't even know.

People from around the world were visiting that city. They heard the noise and rushed to see what was happening. "How can this be?" they asked. "These people are talking in our languages. We can understand what they are saying!"

Peter stepped up and told the crowd the good news about Jesus. "Jesus is alive again!" he said. "God has sent the Holy Spirit. If you turn away from your sins and turn to Jesus, you can be forgiven and have the Holy Spirit too. This is God's promise to all people everywhere."

About three thousand people believed what Peter said and were baptized that day.

Has anyone ever given you a wonderful gift? Jesus gave all His followers a wonderful gift when He sent the Holy Spirit. Jesus didn't want to leave us all alone. He knew we would need strength and power to live God's way after He had gone back to heaven. The Spirit is always with us, so we are never alone! He helps us do what's right. He helps us tell others about Jesus, our wonderful Savior, too!

- When you feel lonely, what do you do?

- How do you think you would feel if you were in the room with Jesus' disciples when the Holy Spirit came?

Dear God, thank You for the power of Your Holy Spirit. Thank You that Jesus sent the Spirit for everyone who believes in Him, even me! Amen.

Do some push-ups, sit-ups, and jumping jacks. Exercise makes our bodies strong. The Holy Spirit makes our spirits strong and helps us do what's right.

• • • • • • • • •

REMEMBER
Jesus gives us power to live for Him.

The Spirit helps us.

—ROMANS 8:26 ICB

WALKING AND LEAPING

ACTS 3

Every day a man who couldn't walk sat beside the temple gate. "Please, could you help me?" he asked people going to the temple. He hoped they would give him some money.

One afternoon Peter and John went to the temple. The man saw them as they walked his way. "Please, could you help me?" he asked them.

"Look at us," Peter said.

The man looked up, expecting money. But no coins *plink-plinked* into his cup.

"I don't have any silver or gold," Peter said. "But I will give you what I *do* have. In the name of Jesus Christ, stand up and walk!" Peter took the man by the hand to help him up. Right away, the man knew his feet and ankles were strong and well.

The man leaped up. **Wow!** He stood! He walked! Then he went into the temple with Peter and John—walking, leaping, and praising God! Hallelujah!

THINK AND TALK

What's your favorite way to play outdoors or your favorite indoor sport? Do you like to run? Jump? Climb? Kick or throw a ball? Imagine if you couldn't do those things. The man who couldn't walk didn't think he could ever be healed. He asked for money, but he got something much better because of the power of Jesus' name.

- When are some times that you need help?

- How could the power of Jesus' name help you when those things happen?

Dear God, thank You for the power of Jesus' name. Help me call to Jesus whenever I need help. Amen.

Say a cheer for Jesus. You can learn this cheer or make up one of your own. You can also make up motions to go with the words.

Jesus, Jesus, He's the best!
He is stronger than the rest!
When we call on Jesus' name,
We will never be the same!
J . . . E . . . S-U-S! Yaaaay, Jesus!

• • • • • • • •

REMEMBER
Jesus' name has power.

Believe in the name of . . . Jesus.

—1 John 3:23 ESV

PAUL'S BIG SURPRISE

ACTS 9

Paul had a goal: find Christians and hurt them! Paul didn't believe in Jesus. But on the road to Damascus, he got a big surprise.

Bam! A light from heaven shone around Paul. He fell to the ground. He heard a voice say, "Paul, why are you hurting Me?"

"Who are You?" Paul asked.

"I am Jesus," said the voice. "Get up and go into the city now. You will be told what you must do."

Paul stood up. He couldn't see! So his friends led him into the city. He stayed there for three days, but he was still blind and didn't eat or drink anything the whole time.

A man named Ananias came to see Paul. "The Lord Jesus sent me here," said Ananias. "He wants you to have your sight back." Ananias put his hands on Paul's shoulders, and Paul could see again! He was baptized right away.

Paul became a Christian and had a new life—teaching and preaching about Jesus wherever he went.

Paul tried to hurt Jesus' followers, but Jesus changed Paul and gave him important work to do—telling others about Jesus and starting new churches. We all can change from bad to good when Jesus gives us new life!

- **What is the brightest light you've ever seen?**

- **What kind of work can you do for Jesus?**

> Dear God, I'm glad I can do important work for Jesus. Teach me what to do. Amen.

Do you know someone who is blind? What would it feel like to be blind? Ask a grown-up to cover your eyes with a scarf and then lead you around the house. Do you know where you are? How do you feel? Talk about how Paul felt when he couldn't see.

• • • • ● ● ● • • •

REMEMBER
Jesus changes us.

Anyone who belongs to Christ has become a new person.

—2 Corinthians 5:17 NLT

BEST DRESSED

ACTS 9

In the city of Joppa a believer named Dorcas was always doing kind things for people and helping the poor. One of the ways Dorcas helped was sewing new clothes. With fabric, needles, and thread, Dorcas made dresses, tunics, and coats. **Snip and stitch, snip and stitch!** Dorcas gave the clothes she made to people who needed them—boys and girls, moms and dads, grandmas and grandpas.

Then Dorcas became very sick, and she died. Her church friends were sad, and they called one of the church leaders, Peter, to come to Joppa. When he got there, everyone was crying because Dorcas had died, and they showed him the coats and other clothes that Dorcas made to give to others.

Peter asked everyone to leave the room. He knelt down by Dorcas's body and prayed for Jesus' power to make Dorcas alive again. Then he said, "Dorcas, get up." Dorcas opened her eyes, and when she saw Peter, she sat up. She was alive again! Now she could keep on doing kind deeds and making clothes for many people.

We love others and help them because they matter to Jesus. Doing kind and helpful deeds for others is one way we can show them Jesus' love.

- What is something you've done to help others in need?

- When you help someone in need, how do you feel?

Dear God, thank You that I can help others in need as Dorcas did. I want to show Jesus' love to others! Amen.

As a family, choose a way to help others in need this week. Make a plan and make it happen. Some ideas are donating books and toys you've outgrown to a women's shelter, doing yard work for an elderly or sick neighbor, taking flowers to a nursing home, or volunteering at an animal shelter.

• • • ● ● ● • • •

REMEMBER
Jesus wants us to help others.

Share with those in need.

—Ephesians 4:28 NIV

SET FREE

ACTS 12

196

Peter was in prison for preaching about Jesus. At night he slept chained between two soldiers.

One night a bright light appeared in the prison cell. An angel stood in front of Peter and woke him up. "Peter, quick! Get up!" the angel said.

Clank! Peter's chains fell off. The guards kept sleeping.

"Get dressed! Put on your shoes!" the angel said.

Peter did what he was told. The guards snored on.

"Now put on your coat and follow me," the angel said.

Peter thought he was dreaming. He followed the angel down the hall. None of the guards saw him! **Crrreak!** The big iron gate opened by itself. Peter walked outside with the angel. They started down the street, and suddenly the angel disappeared.

"I'm *not* dreaming!" Peter said. "God sent an angel to set me free!" He hurried to find his church friends who had been praying for him.

Jesus always knows what is going on with us. He cares about everything that happens to us. When bad things happen, He will help us—sometimes in the most surprising ways!

- What are some ways Jesus shows He cares about you?

- When Peter was in prison, his friends were praying for him. Who needs your prayers today?

> Dear God, I'm glad Jesus cares about me and helps me. Thank You for Jesus! Amen.

Make paper chains with strips of construction paper and tape. Wrap the chains around your feet and wrists, and ask someone to fasten them so they won't fall off. Then pretend to be Peter in prison when the angel appeared. Unfasten your chains and let them fall right off!

· · •●●●● · ··

REMEMBER
Jesus helps us.

He cares for you.

—1 Peter 5:7 ICB

TRUE
BELIEVER

ACTS 16

Paul and his friend Silas traveled from town to town, telling people the **good news** about Jesus *and* that Jesus came not just for the Jewish people but for everyone! (People who weren't Jewish were called *Gentiles*.)

On a Sabbath day in Philippi, some women met outside the city, near a river, to pray. One of them was Lydia, a wealthy businesswoman. She was a Gentile who worshipped God but hadn't yet heard the good news.

Paul and Silas had come to Philippi, and on that same Sabbath they went looking for a place for prayer. They saw the women at the river and asked to join them and speak with them. Paul told the women the **good news** about Jesus.

Lydia listened carefully to what Paul said, and as she listened, God opened her heart to believe that what Paul said was true. She was baptized along with everyone in her household. Then she said to Paul and Silas, "If you know I am a true believer in the Lord, stay here in my home as my guests." And so they did.

The good news about Jesus is for everyone, and everyone needs to hear it. When we become believers and follow Jesus, we have work to do! We can tell people about Jesus' love for them, and we can do kind deeds to help the workers who tell about Jesus in faraway places.

- Who teaches you the good news about Jesus and His love for you? How can you thank or help them?

- Do you know any missionaries? What can you do to support their work?

> Dear God, thank You that the good news about Jesus is for everyone! Help me share the good news with people who need to hear it. Amen.

On a world map, mark a place where you can share the good news now—the city or town where you live. Think about places you might want to go to tell about Jesus when you are older. If your church supports mission work around the world, mark those places on the map too and pray for those efforts as a family this week.

• • • • • • • • •

REMEMBER
Jesus wants us to share the good news.

"Make disciples of all nations."

—MATTHEW 28:19 NIV

SHIPWRECKED

ACTS 27–28

God sent Paul to Rome on a big sailing ship. On the way, the ship ran into a terrible storm. Wind, waves, and rain hid the sun and the stars.

The sailors gave up hope, but Paul said, "Have courage! God is taking care of us. He sent an angel to me last night. The angel said we will be shipwrecked on an island, but we will all live."

Finally, the ship neared land. Paul encouraged the sailors to eat. They hadn't eaten anything for a long time. "You have been so worried," he said. "Please eat now, for your own good."

The sailors tried to sail to land, but waves hit the ship and broke it to pieces. **Smash!** Some sailors swam toward the island. Others floated on boards from the ship. Everyone reached land safely.

Crackle! Pop! The people on the island welcomed the sailors with a big bonfire. Paul stayed on the island until spring. Then he set sail for Rome on a different ship.

Paul knew God wanted him to go to Rome to preach about Jesus, and he knew Jesus would help him get there. So Paul could have courage and not be afraid, even though being in the storm and getting shipwrecked was hard. When you know Jesus wants you to do something hard, you can have courage too!

- When is a time you have needed to be brave?

- Why does it sometimes take courage to do the right thing?

Dear God, thank You for Paul's example of courage. Help me depend on Jesus and be brave too. Amen.

GREEN MEANS GO!

Act out with a grown-up how you will show your courage
the next time you want to be brave. Here are some ideas:
What will you do when you get a shot at the doctor's
office, when you want to be a friend to someone no
one else likes, or when friends want you to cheat to win
a game?

• • • • • • •

REMEMBER
Jesus gives us courage.

"Have courage! . . . Don't be afraid."

—MATTHEW 14:27 ICB

GREAT DAY!

1 THESSALONIANS 4; REVELATION 21–22

God gave the apostle John a wonderful peek at the beautiful home in heaven where we will live someday.

The city shines like a sparkling jewel because God is there. Everything in the city is made of gold as pure as glass. Around the city stands a tall wall with twelve gates. Each gate is a single perfect pearl.

The river of the water of life flows through the city from the throne of God and Jesus. The tree of life is there too, with twelve different kinds of fruit.

There is no sun and no moon, no day and no night. Jesus gives the city light. God will live with us in the city. We will be His people, and He will be our God. There will be no sadness or crying. Everything will be new!

At the right time, Jesus will come from heaven on the clouds with a loud **shout!** and a trumpet **blast!** He is the One whom God promised would make things right again. Everyone will see Him! Everyone who loves Him will rise up to meet Him in the air. Jesus will take us to our new home in heaven. What a great day that will be!

We don't know when Jesus will come back, but we don't need to worry about it—we just need to be ready. We get ready by loving Jesus and other people the way He wants us to. We don't know exactly what heaven will be like, but we know it will be good!

- Have you ever waited a long time for someone to come to visit? Who was it? Was it hard to wait?

- How do you feel when someone you love comes to see you?

> Dear God, help me to be ready when Jesus comes back. Thank You for Jesus and our new home someday in heaven with You. Amen.

Draw a picture of what you imagine heaven will look like. Decorate your picture with glitter, sequins, or shiny stickers. Heaven will be a beautiful place!

· · ● ● ◗ ● ● · ·

REMEMBER
Jesus will take us to our forever home someday.

Amen. Come, Lord Jesus!

—Revelation 22:20 icb

ABOUT THE AUTHOR

 **Diane Stortz** writes for children and adults with the goal of making God's wonders known to the next generation.

She clearly remembers the moment in first-grade reading circle when reading "clicked" for her. She wants children everywhere to learn to love reading God's Word as much as she does today.

Diane and her husband, Ed, are parents of two daughters and have five grandchildren—all boys!

 **Hannah Marks** was born in 1977 in Derby, England, UK. She grew up in the Midlands and now lives in Hertfordshire with her husband, children, and a (bonkers) kitten. She's self-taught and often draws inspiration from anything vintage as well as completely random thoughts that drop into her head, which usually happens after eating cake. Hannah works digitally in Corel Painter and Photoshop, creating characters and illustrations and using patterns and textures to make everything look fancy.